Creating a Transnational Space in the First Year Writing Classroom

Edited by

W. Ordeman

University of North Texas

Series in Literary Studies

VERNON PRESS

www.vernonpress.com

In the Americas:
Vernon Press
1000 N West Street, Suite 1200
Wilmington, Delaware, 19801
United States

In the rest of the world:
Vernon Press
C/Sancti Espiritu 17,
Malaga, 29006
Spain

Series in Literary Studies

Library of Congress Control Number: 2020949840

ISBN: 978-1-64889-302-5

Also available: 978-1-62273-952-3 [Hardback]; 978-1-64889-204-2 [PDF, E-Book]

Cover design by Vernon Press using elements designed by Freepik.

Table of contents

List of figures and tables

Abstract

The chapters in this volume offer new ways of thinking about and applying theories of transnational rhetoric in first-year composition classrooms. Transnationalism is still a rather nascent field in rhetorical studies, and the growing body of literature has thus far focused on the critical necessity of laying theoretical groundwork. There remains a lack of applied pedagogical research teachers can use to help create and nurture transnational spaces in the classroom. While several works in this volume contribute to our understanding of the breadth and depth of transnational rhetoric, the goal of this work is to offer applicable pedagogy that helps create and nurture transnational spaces within a specific writing context.

Introduction

Theoretical Groundwork

What do we mean by "transnationalism"? In her article, *What's the Difference Between "Translingual" and "Transnational" Composition?: Clarifying the Relationship between two Terms*, Carrie Kilfoil claims that these terms can often seem synonymous and that understanding their nuance requires intentional study. Still, it's not uncommon to hear the terms interchangeably. After all, aren't all translinguals also transnationals (and vice versa)? Don't both denote the blending of culture ideologies? Part of this confusion, Kilfoil claims, stems from citizens of monolingual societies presuming all nations are monolingual entities. It is true that many nations represent monolingual societies - some even creating laws to enforce monolingualism (such as the English Only movement), and nation states have used linguistic colonization to subjugate translingual communities (see Anzaldúa). But as Yasemin Yildiz has argued, there is a false assumption that "individuals and social formations...possess one 'true' language (their 'mother tongue') and through this possession [are] organically linked to an exclusive, clearly demarcated ethnicity, culture, and nation" (2). While translingual communities represent identities informed by language with multiple languages represented in a single community, a transnational perspective, as Yildiz puts it, "puts the emphasis on human agency: such groups are the result of cross-border activities which link individuals, families and local groups" (2). Using transnational and translingual interchangeably reinforces a limited definition of rhetoric - that it is a strictly linguistic act. It is important that students and faculty obtain a framework for understanding spaces where national interest and national identities are concurrent with but exist apart from language.

In 2008, Hesford and Schell argued "all national formations are constructed within and often solidified by transnational connectivities" (464) and called for research in composition studies that recognizes these transnational connectivities. The following year, Christiane Donahue re-iterated this when she called more "deep intercultural awareness" to avoid "efforts [that] will remain stuck in a-historical, a-contextual, and highly partial modes of intellectual tourism." (236) Since then, discourse in transnationalism composition has begun to address these relationships and lay theoretical groundwork for further study.

The introduction to the recent *Transnationalism: Theory, History, and Practice* edited by Xiaoye You argues the foundation of transnationalism consists of translingualism, transculturalism, and cosmopolitanism – each having a distinct role in our conception of transnationalism. This foundation has been partly constructed by research mentioned above and discourse on related areas including immigrant and migrant studies (Pandey; Simon; Vieira), digital literacy (Berry et al.; Lam and Rosario-Ramos), and globalization in higher education (Kang; Lorimer Leonard; McNamara) and transnational feminist studies (Dingo). The works of these individuals suggest transnational rhetoric create transnational space - begging the question, how do these created spaces influence agents therein?

Encouraging translingual practice in the classroom is crucial to empower students to influence and recognize influence within their environments. Language has no doubt affected the transnational composition classrooms, but as Xiaoye You has argued and the authors in this volume point out, translingualism functions as the predicate of transnational pedagogy which deserves to be seen as an independent agent (*Transnationalism: Theory, History, and Practice*). Understanding the relationship of these two ideologies not only helps teachers develop pedagogy that creates space for developing and examining transnationalism and translingualism independently, it will also reaffirm to our students the threshold concepts we believe about writing.

Answering the Call

Teaching writing within these transnational spaces helps foster what Rebecca Lorimer Leonard calls *rhetorical attunement:* "an understanding that assumes multiplicity and invites the negotiation of meaning across difference" ("Multilingual Writing as Rhetorical Attunement"288). Sara Alvarez claims transnational writers can "sustain and foster transnational literacies and networks via various forms of writing that are of value to the academy" (344). This volume responds to this assertion. Each chapter addresses one of the following questions: "How can we use the resources at our disposal to incorporate transnational ecologies in homogeneous classrooms?" and/or "What can be done to foster transnational literacies and networks as a direct response to transnational spaces outside the classroom?" All authors see transnational space in the classroom as an opportunity to help students see rhetoric as highly contextual and subject to the agents involved. David S. Martin's recent work, *Transnational Writing Program Administration*, has helped illuminate long-standing assumptions about program curriculum and pedagogy within writing programs. This volume continues in research that understands "transnational activities are thoroughly shifting the questions we ask about writing curricula, the space and place in which writing happens, and the cultural and linguistic issues at the heart of the relationships forged in literacy work" (Martins 1).

This volume also addresses Leonard's call in her short essay "Moving Beyond Methodological Nationalism" when she calls for research that is "more precise and less restricted." (129) Readers will find precision for the term transnationalism through the specific pedagogical projects each author has introduced in their classes. Restrictions in terms of correct/appropriate/ right and incorrect/inappropriate/wrong are guided by each author's specific pedagogical goal.

Several authors in this volume were afforded the opportunity to teach rhetoric to students who live in *transnational spaces* where the rhetoric is reflective of an altogether unique phenomenon happening outside the classroom. The authors share their analysis and results in an effort to find effective teaching methods that satisfy student learning outcomes while creating ecologies that reflect the values and perspectives of the students in the room. Other authors in this volume teach in homogeneous classrooms (classrooms where one cultural group accounts for the majority of the students) where they themselves bring a representation of transnationalism by teaching English writing courses as a non-native speaker of English. Their purpose is not so much to reflect the ecologies of the students' transnationalism, but rather to reveal the transnational spaces they as instructors create. Translingualism is a common theme throughout the work as translingual pedagogies are commonly used to help construct/reflect transnational ecologies. As both are still relatively novel pedagogical approaches, there are a number of new ways of analyzing, implementing, and evaluating their pedagogy.

Where previous work on transnational pedagogy has focused on theory, the goal of this volume is to offer examples of transnational pedagogy *in action* followed by discussions of what these applications imply to our understanding of the field. By building a larger database of transnational pedagogy, teachers will better be able to develop writing curricula that create transnational space - a space many students and teachers are already living and operating in.

Chapter Sections

All the authors in this volume are connected by their shared vision of cultivating transnational spaces in the first-year writing classrooms. They write to cross the border between scholarship on transnationalism as rhetorical theory and applying this theory to first-year writing curriculum and pedagogy. *Creating a Transnational Space in the First Year Writing Classroom* is structured along the border of pedagogical research methods and classroom application and thus divided into three sections based on the author's implementation and research methodology. The chapters are divided into these sections to help align the reader's goals with correlating goals of the authors. Researchers who are most interested in understanding their students' relationship with transnationalism might find the chapters in Part 1 most beneficial as they incorporate ethnographic research. Readers who are in a position to create transnational courses study might find chapters in Part 2 most helpful. Educators who are interested in applying a piece-meal approach might find the chapters in Part 3 helpful as they are concerned with specific assignments. By dividing the work thus, readers can guide themselves toward sections most pertinent to their objectives.

Creating Transnational Spaces through Ethnographic Reflection

The authors of this section use ethnographic reflections as a means of both evaluating and then inventing new pedagogical models. Their qualitative approach to research begins without a materialized hypothesis and is facilitated by inductive reasoning allowing them to discover insights specific to where they teach. These teachers explore first-year writing pedagogies via collecting qualitative data through the ethnographies of the students. Norma Dibrell begins her inquiry without asking specific questions, but rather from a position of understanding the students' experience outside the classroom. She uses their reflections as a means of challenging constructs of linguistic homogeneity. Abu Saleh Mohammad Rafi and Anne-Marie Morgan, on the other hand, begin by asking three open-ended questions specific to the efficacy of Rafi's classroom – one that is a transnational ecology. He uses several methods of gathering qualitative data to assess the efficacy of his teaching methods. Naoko Akai-Dennis' research begins by questioning assumptions about agency in transnational spaces. Akai-Dennis has her students collect data of language-use outside the classroom and uses the students' ethnographies to highlight the shortcomings of current theoretical constructs of translingual contact zones. All three authors undertake their research in the understanding that, as with most novel fields of research, not all of the "appropriate" questions have been conceived. Sometimes, an instructor has a vision for where they are going but lacks the fundamental inquiries that will drive progress. Similarly, the authors in this section first offer a literary synthesis as a means of providing the reader with their vision, and then offer ethnographic data as a means of validating and/or invalidating fundamental claims made by the theory of transnationalism.

Creating Transnational Spaces through Course Design focused on Genre

In this section, authors conduct their research by designing course content and course materials that emphasize genre. They do so in order to foster ideas of transnational spaces through classroom discourse, classroom activities, and writing prompts. The roles of the authors in this section include Writing Program Administrators, Professors, and Graduate Teachers of Record, giving the reader a unique perspective of how one can create transnational spaces based on their professional level of influence. Andrew Hollinger and Colin Charlton are writing program directors at a Hispanic Serving Institution (HSI) where transnationals make up the majority of their student body. Their program is designed around *writing about writing* curriculum through transnational writing environments. Asmita Ghimire shares her insight as a transnational graduate assistant in a predominately homogeneous environment. She and Elizabethada Wright have built their transnational curriculum to address this type of dichotomy. Demet Yigitbilek shares a similar experience as the graduate teacher of record in a university in the midwest. She designed the course *Language and/as Identity* and uses her transnational experience to teach genre in her rhetoric classroom. All these authors offer reflections that are particularly helpful for course/program designers who are looking for research that includes comprehensive implementation of transnational pedagogies.

Creating Transnational Spaces through Assignment Design

Authors of this section use specific assignments as a means of incorporating transnational pedagogy for specific course modules within a first-year writing course. Their aim is to create transnational spaces within their classrooms to achieve specific learning outcomes in addition to those common to first-year composition courses. Maria Houston and Ekaterina Gradaleva's chapter specifically studies the efficacy of a transnational composition assignment that teaches digital literacies as well as collaborative writing. Authors Phuong Minh Tran, Kyle J. Lucas, and Kenneth Tanemura synthesize data collected from numerous transnational composition assignments to compare their successes and failures and offer suggestions to instructors on how they can be used to create transnational spaces.

W. Ordeman
January 2020

Works Cited

Alvarez, Sara P. "Multilingual Writers in College Contexts." *Journal of Adolescent & Adult Literacy*, vol. 62, 2018, pp. 342-345.

Anzaldúa, Gloria. *Borderlands: The New Mestiza = La Frontera.* 1st ed. San Francisco: Aunt Lute, 1987.

Berry, Patrick W., et al. Transnational Literate Lives in Digital Times. Computers and Composition Digital P/Utah State UP, 2012.

Dingo, Rebecca. *Networking Arguments: Rhetoric, Transnational Feminism, and Public Policy Writing.* University of Pittsburgh Press, 2012.

Donahue, Christiane. "'Internationalization' and Composition Studies: Reorienting the Discourse." *College Composition and Communication* 61.2 (2009): 212–243.

Hall, Stuart. "Subjects in History: Making Diasporic Identities." *The House That Race Built: Black Americans, U.S. Terrain.* edited by Wahneema Lubiano, Pantheon, 1997. Pp. 289-300.

Hesford, Wendy S., and Eileen E. Schell. "Introduction: Configurations of Transnationality: Locating Feminist Rhetorics." *College English* 70.5 (2008): 461–470.

Kang, Yu-Kyung. "Tensions of Local and Global: South Korean International Students Navigating and Maximizing US College Life." Literacy in Composition Studies, vol. 3, no. 3, 2015.

Kilfoil, Carrie. "What's the Difference Between 'Translingual' and 'Transnational' Composition?: Clarifying the Relationship between two Terms." *Transnational Writing.* Transnationalwriting.wordpress.com, Sept. 6 2016.

Lam, Wan Shun Eva., and Enid Rosario-Ramos. "Multilingual Literacies in Transnationally Digitally Mediated Contexts: An Exploratory Study of Immigrant Teens in the United States." Language and Education, vol. 23, no. 2, 2009, pp. 171-90.

Leonard, Rebecca Lorimer. "Multilingual Writing as Rhetorical Attunement." College English, vol. 76, no. 3, 2014, pp. 227–247. JSTOR, www.jstor.org/stable/24238241. Accessed 3 Oct. 2020.

—. "Where We Are: The 'Global Turn' and Its Implications for Composition." *Composition Studies*, vol. 44, no. 1, Mar. 2016, pp. 127–130.

Martins, David S., editor. *Transnational Writing Program Administration.* Utah State University Press, 2015.

McNamara, Tom. "Diminishing Returns at Corporate U: Chinese Undergraduates and Composition's Activist Legacy." Literacy in Composition Studies, vol. 6, no. 1, 2018.

Pandey, Iswari. *South Asian in the Mid-South: Migrations of Literacies.* U of Pittsburgh P, 2015.

Simon, Kaia. "Daughters Learning from Fathers: Migrant Family Literacies that Mediate Borders." Literacy in Composition Studies, vol. 5, no. 1, 2017.

Vieira, Kate. *American by Paper: How Documents Matter in Immigrant Literacy.* U of Minnesota P, 2016.

Yildiz, Yasemin. *Beyond the Mother Tongue: The Postmonolingual Condition.* New York: Fordham University Press, 2012. Print.

You, Xiaoye, editor. *Transnational Writing Education.* New York: Routledge, 2018.

Part 1.
Creating Transnational Spaces through Ethnographic Reflections

In the following chapters, authors Norma Dibrell, Abu Saleh Mohammad Rafi and Anne-Marie Morgan, and Naoko Akai-Dennis share results from their ethnographic research of implemented transnational pedagogy. As is common in transnational pedagogy, the authors use translingual curriculum as a means of cultivating reflections on the students in their unique transnational environments. Norma Dibrell's objective is stated explicitly in the opening paragraph of her chapter, *Erasing the Idea of Monolingual Students in Translingual Spaces: A Study of Translingual Pedagogy in First-Year Writing*. She believes the purpose of first-year writing is to equip students with skills to communicate and "to equalize society." How does transnational pedagogy fulfill these purposes? The answer lies in the unique ecology of Dibrell's university which lies along the United States-Mexico border. In her literary review, she synthesizes theories by Carnagarajah, Horner, and García and offers readers a unique insight into how these theories are perceived and analyzed by freshman transnational students. Dibrell's aspirations of making her classroom a fair place for her students is realized through a pedagogy informed by the students' experience outside the classroom.

Abu Saleh Mohammad Rafi and Anne-Marie Morgan's chapter, *Translanguaging and Academic Writing: Possibilities and Challenges in English-only Classrooms*, uses a similar methodology. The authors incorporate translingual pedagogies in transnational classrooms as a means of improving a student learning outcome provided by the institution: to teach students how to speak and write in "Standard English." Rafi and Morgan's work analyzes data through Bakhtin's notion of heteroglossia which emphasizes the synthesis of seemingly disparate data sets. Their approach is used to analyze the tension between an "English only" policy and the transnational classroom by collecting data from student-researcher interaction and student work examples. The authors provide a literary synthesis from theorists such as Carnagarajah, Horner, García, Karimba, and others as groundwork for their investigation. The authors use ethnographic data to reflect on the outcomes of transnational classroom design. Like Dibrell, they teach from English in a transnational setting. Though the university is located in Bangladesh, it had formerly banned the use of languages other than English in the classroom. Rafi and Morgan's classroom is distinct from Dibrell's in that it is designed to teach English proficiency rather than composition, but the three researchers arrived at similar transnational pedagogical means to achieve their goal.

In *Language, Home, and Transnational Space,* Naoko Akai-Dennis examines different ideas of transnational spaces outside the classroom to reimagine social spaces for translingual pedagogy. She calls into question claims concerning contact zones and translingual agents creating transnational spaces. She unpacks theories made by Mary Louisa Pratt, Canagarajah, Pennycook, García, Wei, and Derrida to investigate how translingual students function in transnational spaces. Akai-Dennis builds a class based on Anzaldúa's works only to realize by reviewing qualitative data collected by her students that some contact zones are not preconditions for translingual practices, and therefore cannot be transformed into transnational spaces. Juxtaposing translingual theorists with Derrida's ideas of the fluidity between self and language, Akai-Dennis' research suggests that contact zones are not completely generative as others claim. Instead, they are dependent on levels of influence from existing agents of power. To create transnational spaces, Akai-Dennis argues we must work to erase agents of power who marginalize translinguals.

These chapters add value to transnational pedagogy by illustrating how ethnographic data can evaluate the efficacy of translingual theories in creating transnational spaces. Dibrell focuses specifically on qualitative research in her students' reading reflections and a *Reflective Essay* in which students reflect on the shifting perspectives and novel constructs from their first day in class to the last. Rafi and Morgan's data is an aggregate of classroom observations, pedagogical inventions, focus group discussions, and an interview with the course tutor. Akai-Dennis' chapter provides logs of student interactions occurring outside the classroom.

Though learning outcomes and purposes differ, the authors demonstrate the value of in-class reflections when evaluating student learning objectives. Ethnographic approaches are specifically helpful in pedagogical research as they can act as methods of research as well as reflective exercises for students' metacognition.

Chapter 1

Erasing the Idea of Monolingual Students in Translingual Spaces: A Study of Translingual Pedagogy in First-Year Writing

Norma Denae Dibrell

University of Texas Rio Grande Valley

Abstract: If the goal of First-Year Writing courses (FYW) is to equip students will skills and knowledge and habits that can make them better writers and thinkers and communications, and if education is going to be seen as an equalizer in society, then pedagogy must reflect that. Students do not always process information and make meaning in English. The pedagogy used to teach students should meet the needs of the students. Ofelia García explains how translanguaging pedagogies can serve different purposes in the classroom, two of them being "to assist and motivate learning, and deepen meaning, understandings and knowledge" and "for greater metalinguistic awareness and linguistic consciousness, including critical sociolinguistic consciousness" ("Translanguaging in Schools" 262). If educators are thinking predominately about FYW classes, their goal should be to allow students to become better writers, and with that comes being a better reader, thinker, processor, and communicator. It is unfair that only students who use SAE comfortably benefit from FYW courses. In The Rio Grande Valley, instructors of FYW understand the needs of our students. And because of this, not just in the RGV, but everywhere, writing teachers cannot continue to teach FYW for the SAE speaking majority. This translingual pedagogy, this acceptance of language and identity diversity in the classroom is a key lever in making education a key for success for our students instead of keeping it as another form of systemic oppression. This chapter explores student end of semester reflections and student reading reflections to investigate how using a translingual pedagogy in the FYW classroom affects student meaning making and sociolinguistic consciousness.

Keywords: translingual pedagogy, First-Year Writing (FYW), translanguaging, language diversity, sociolinguistics

***

Introduction

If the goal of First-Year Writing courses (FYW) is to equip students with skills, knowledge, and habits that can make them better writers, thinkers, and communications, and if education is going to be seen as an equalizer in society, then our pedagogy must reflect that.

Translanguaging pedagogies can serve different purposes in the classroom, two of them being "to assist and motivate learning, and deepen meaning, understandings and knowledge" and to create spaces "for greater metalinguistic awareness and linguistic consciousness, including critical sociolinguistic consciousness" (García, "Translanguaging in Schools," 261). The pedagogy used to teach students should meet the needs of the students. And the truth is, students do not always process information and make meaning in English. If we are thinking predominately about FYW classes, our goal should be to allow students to become better writers, and with that comes being a better reader, thinker, processor, and communicator. It is unfair that only students who use Standard Edited American English (SEAE) comfortably benefit from FYW courses.

In The Rio Grande Valley, we understand the needs of our students. Most, if not all, of our students are what many will call bilingual (a mixture of English and Spanish language knowledge). Our campus is split into two separate campuses that are over 60 miles apart (one campus is less than a mile from the US- Mexico Border). Many students commute from border towns in Mexico where they live to the campus they attend in the US. It's not just the languages that inform how they learn and make meaning, but the cultures, the spaces, the literal borders they cross daily. And because of this, not just in the RGV, but everywhere, we cannot continue to teach FYW for the SAE speaking majority. This translingual pedagogy, this acceptance of language and identity diversity in the classroom is a key lever in making education accessible to all. As a native of the Rio Grande Valley, and a biracial Hispanic woman, who has lived her life both fascinated by the language use in the region and feeling caught between the languages and cultures, I feel that as a teacher in this space, it is my duty to foster environments where our specific and unique language use is challenged, embraced, and explored.

In this chapter, I will explore students' end-of-semester reflections and students' reading reflections to investigate how using a translingual pedagogy in the FYW classroom affects student meaning-making and sociolinguistic consciousness.

Transfer and translingualism allows us to account for language diversity in the classroom and see it as a benefit instead of a drawback. When I think of my L2 students and how they are able to articulate such profound arguments and make connections in my class, I have to admit that for my L2 (second language) learners, these realizations are made mostly, if not completely, in Spanish. When I limit them to English by only allowing or grading English in the classroom on assignments, or ask them to translate their thought to English (after they have done it in Spanish), they struggle. They feel like all the insightful comments they made in Spanish are not valuable. My goal as an educator is to ensure that students feel that their critical thinking capabilities are valuable in any language and that what matters are the connections and the meanings they make. Translingualism gives me a pedagogy and rationale to follow to make this a reality in my classroom.

Literature Review

There has been an assortment of in-depth research conducted on translingualism. Based on how I'd like to frame translingual pedagogy as an accessible and necessary tool in the FYW classroom, I chose to organize my literature review by first framing my argument in terms of decolonial theory and standard language ideology then by explaining how I will use "language."

Walter Mignolo argues that the literacy of the Americas was colonized based on how Europeans forced the indigenous people to use their alphabet and their languages. I argue that, to this day, we are using standard language ideology to keep non-SEAE speakers oppressed. We must acknowledge that "throughout the history of humankind, conquerors have inflicted their language on the conquered" (Mignolo 30). This is still happening. Specifically, in the writing classroom, we expect students to write grammatical, syntactical essays in SEAE. This form of oppression is interfering with student learning. Not only do we force students to use a certain kind of language, but we also force them to make meaning in certain ways, based on the values we show as educators, having them read certain articles, grading assignments based on certain criteria, and not valuing the process of creating meaning in different ways, perhaps using different languages.

Before we look at how people use language and how they write, I will give background as to how I will discuss "language" in this paper. The way Canagarajah describe language, like English, "derives from the dominant assumptions of linguistics, informed by the modernist philosophical movement and intellectual culture in which they developed. To begin with, the field treats language as a thing in itself, an objective, identifiable product" (Canagarajah, "Lingua Franca" 934). But language isn't just a product. It's not just an alphabet. It's not just words. It's the words and the ideas and the associations and the meanings we make using language. Language is what we think in, how we communicate, and, of course, how we write.

Translingual theory encourages us "to merge different language resources in situated interactions for new meaning construction" (Canagarajah, "Translingual Practice" 1–2). We use language as part of how we create meaning. In border communities, meaning is made in multiple languages. As Canagarajah states, "translingual practices are widely practiced in communities and everyday community contexts... [but are] ignored or suppressed in classrooms" (4). When we talk about language in a classroom in the United States, we assume we are speaking about something that happened in English, even though we know that many people speak languages other than English. Canagarajah also states that "the translingual orientation posits that while language resources are mobile, they acquire labels and identities through situated uses in particular contexts and get reified through language ideologies" (15). We give meanings to certain ideas and visuals and sounds based on our ideologies and cultures. So this idea of communicating and making-meaning out of what we do is how I categorize language. Language cannot be separated from the environment I learned it in or the way I felt when I used it or the face I'm supposed to make when I say it or where my eyes should be when I make the sound. It's all of it together.

Tranlingualism is the idea that language difference is seen as a resource and not as a barrier (Horner et al.). The theory of translingualism "incorporates the view that all language users, or languagers, are perpetually producing and experimenting with multiple varieties of language" which is important to note not just multilingual students, but also for students who speak many Englishes (Gilyard 284). Technology, social media, and varying discourse communities constantly cause us to shift our language usage and experiment with how to navigate language. While translingualism is a theory that informs how students and teachers should be open to engage with multiple language resources, translanguaging "refers to the development of a speaker's full linguistic repertoire, which does not in any way correspond to the socially and politically defined language of named languages" (García and Kleyn 14). The translingual orientation prepares teachers to engage with students who translanguage and to translanguage themselves. By translanguaging in class, students and teachers are pulling from all of the resources, language, visuals, etc, to make meaning and make connections. They are not limited to certain languages. This is different from bilingilism and code switching, where certain phrases are translated or just repeated in different langauges. Ofelia García described 'dynamic bilingualism' as switching between different languages constantly, almost like you're not switching because you're just thinking how it is natural to you. This is very similar to what Canagarajah calls "performative competence," where you perform the language that you feel you need at a specific time ("Lingua Franca" 9). Translanguaging doesn't require translation. To understand how it works, we look specifically at translanguaging events. A "translanguaging event [is a] multilingual collaborative practice [of] shuttling between languages while responding to texts and situated in local contexts involving emergent bilinguals" (Alvarez 330). These events allow students to work together while translanguaging to make meaning. Translanguaging is differentiated from translingualism by Wei and García because, they argue, while translinualism is a practice and a pedagogy, "translanguaging for us, however, is part of a moral and political act that links the production of alternative meanings to transformative social action. As such, translanguaging contributes to the social justice agenda" (330). Thinking about teachers as social justice advocates, we must think about our students and their identities and respecting them in the classroom. While translingualism follows the same ideology, translanguaging has a more political connotation since language is dynamic and humans pull from all kinds of resources to communicate. As Eli Goldblatt explains, we must "respect people's dignity by creating the conditions for them to be active participants in solving their own problems rather than victims or mere recipients of aid," which, for many students, cannot happen in a strictly monolingual classroom (320). And if we connect this idea of treating all of our students with dignity when it comes to language to transfer from FYW classrooms, we can see that students cannot take ownership of their learning and transfer if they are not able to make meaning and show it. If a student is making meaning and connections in a class or between two classes, but they cannot articulate that connection in English, then we, as educators, have no way of measuring what they are taking away from FYW classes and into other classes. This is where translingualism can come into play. Having a translingual approach in the FYW classroom can encourage more students to share, in the language that they feel comfortable with, what connections and meaning they are making.

The FYW classroom that is currently monoversal in regards to language, culture, and identity can be countered by the idea of a pluriversal classroom. By allowing students to translanguage in the classroom and to write translingually, instructors open up the classroom to this pluriverse of voices that have since been silent.

Language Diversity

Using the translingual approach and embracing language diversity allows students to learn and to be measured regardless if it's in SAE or not, which disrupts the current oppressive system that exists in schools. As educators, we want our students to leave us with more opportunities and connections that they entered our classroom with. Why would we continue to engage in pedagogies that do not allow all of our students the same opportunities?

In FYW classrooms in particular, English is predominately spoken. That does not mean that students prefer that language to think in or to represent themselves. This creates a severe power dynamic between not just teacher and student and among the students themselves, but with each student and their self-worth because students can feel that their language is not the language of school.

To combat this power inequity that comes with using English the way we currently are in schools, García suggests using translanguaging in our pedagogy because it "is precisely a way of ensuring that we view language from the different perspectives that offer us a way to escape the linear upward and restrictive understandings of what language ought to be, opening up *espacios* for different people to act equitably in their worlds through their own languaging" so that students are able to make meaning however they wish and they feel comfortable and know how to use all of their resources (García, "Translanguaging" 256). Translingualism, as a pedagogy, encourages students to make meaning in the language(s) they see fit for the appropriate situation.

Bruce Horner, Min Zhan Lu, Jacqueline Jones Royster, and John Trimbur's foundational piece, *Opinion: Language Difference in Writing: Toward a Translingual Approach*, outlines why we have the need for a "translingual approach" to composition classrooms and describes the theory behind why it should work. They establish the need for a new way to look at language because we have such a variety of students in writing classrooms across the nation and "the Englishes they use vary and multiply" (303).

Because students have not only diverse culture, but diverse languages, even within English, Horner et al. "insists on viewing language differences and fluidities as resources to be preserved, developed and utilized" (304). So, they argue, that instead of seeing all these different languages as a problem in classrooms, we should use it to our advantage (305). Instead of seeing differences in writing as "wrong", we should ask "what the writers are doing with language and why" (305). Horner acknowledges we view differences in language through two equally oppressive lenses. Horner argues that through the translingual approach, "we recognize that we are all language learners" (307). The translingual approach "rejects as both unrealistic and discriminatory" all the language policies and the focuses on grammar (308). In the classroom, the teacher must make it obvious that she is welcoming new and different kinds of language; it is about the "disposition of openness and inquiry" on the teacher's end (311). Horner et al. point out that "Proponents of a translingual approach argue that, in every composition classroom, teachers would do well to address language difference by deemphasizing the importance of arbitrary norms and, instead, aiming to understand and leverage the ways difference is conscripted in service of rhetorical action" (305). To truly have a translingual classroom, instructors should focus on rhetorical actions, audience, and students making-meaning rather than things like grammar and verb tense. This is crucial, especially for L2 learners who may feel like they are not welcome in a classroom because of their language but want to make meaning in the class through the means they can.

Ultimately, by forcing students to think and write and create meaning in academic English, instructors almost forbid them from doing it at all because "only those whose language practices can easily pass through the narrow linguistic passageway that schools construct, have then access to knowledge, knowledge of *ciencia, historia, literatura, matemáticas*, and all other ways of understanding the world" (García "Translanguaging in Schools" 257). Students who do not speak academic English and are not comfortable engaging with it are left out.

To illustrate how translingual pedagogy can impact student learning, I will explore student end of semester reflections and student reading reflections to investigate how using a translingual pedagogy in the FYW classroom affects student meaning-making and sociolinguistic consciousness through identity affirmation. I would like to allow most of the student work to stand on its own, allow their voices to be heard with less of my own opinion.

Through these student reflections, we can see that many of my students had never been given the opportunity to think critically about language and how they use language. The term of translingualism was new to many of them, but the concept was not. They were able, in several instances, to redefine what they saw as "proper" or "acceptable" language used based on the readings and class discussions of translingual theory.

Context

In the Fall of 2018, I taught an English Rhetoric and Composition 1302 course of 25 students, 16 of which commuted to campus from Mexico each day, 21 of which spoke Spanish at home, and 18 of which are more comfortable speaking/thinking in Spanish than English. It was a goal of mine to encourage students to explore their own identity as it related to language in the course. I also made it clear what my positionality was- a white passing Hispanic woman who speaks SEAE, Spanglish, and Spanish. I shared with them by experiences using language in and out of the Rio Grande Valley, growing up in the area, and as a teacher. I hoped that this would spark additional insight as they completed these reflections and analysis.

Student Writing Analysis: Student Reading Reflections

The first set of student writing I'd like to look at are from a reading reflections I gave during the third week of the semester. The prompt was as follows:

Prompt Week 3: Compare Deborah Brandt's "Sponsors of Literacy" with Canagarajah's "Codemeshing in Academic Writing: Identifying Teaching Strategies of Translanguaging.

These quotes that I chose reflect how students began to challenge language dominance and how this affirmed their identity based on the readings. The reading reflections and responses to each other submitted online prior to our in-class discussion of the readings. The students also engage with each other in ways that affirm and challenge the way they are thinking about language.

Student A

"Brandt and Canagarajah's views also align to my language experience as I was brought up in a Hispanic community and family, therefore I am bilingual and would love the have the, "freedom" of code-meshing some Spanish language in my work at school to truly express myself in my writing. After reading Brandt and Canagarajah's views of literacy, I have come to realize that literacy is learned through more powerful figures that help shape it, and that our literacy is always improving and expanding throughout our life."

Student B

"When I was younger my fist language was spanish. I would stuggle in school and had a difficult time in writing and speaking English. I would write my essays in spanish and translate them into english so they would be acceptable to my teachers. Her strategy would have helped my very much and would have given me the opportunity to express myself in a bilingual matter and show what i know and really express myself. I believe this would suggest to give us bilinguals an opportunity to express ourselves in full. At home we do not speak only one language we mix and have fun with both, so why can't we do the same in our writing if it gets out point across and lets our reader know us better."

Student C

In response to Student B: "I agree with you about how people and schools should be letting us write by mixing two languages. So we can express ourselves completely by codemeshing. I was not familiar with the term translanguaging or either codemeshing as well until I read the essay. "Proper" writing isn't always "good" writing in my opinion. Proper writing wouldn't let you codemesh, but people still do it and their writing is still considered good. Then again, it will always depend on who your audience is, but you should write the way you feel would best express you."

Through these student examples of writing, it was clear to me that introducing these concepts so early in the semester was encouraging them to begin challenging dominant language norms that have been enforced both spatially (US/Mexico border) as well as ideologically.

They are able to articulate that they see school as an English place even though they may literally live in another country where English is not used. For instance, Student C makes the argument that ""Proper" writing isn't always "good" writing in my opinion. Proper writing wouldn't let you codemesh, but people still do it and their writing is still considered good." This student was thinking about their specific environment and audience and culture and how they have seen writing happen that challenges the status quo as far as SEAE is concerned, but be good in a certain situation.

These realizations, especially early on the semester, frame how students study writing and see themselves as writers for the rest of the course- allowing them to question what makes writing good and how we language in different contexts.

Student Writing Analysis: End of Semester Reflections

The second assignment I'd like to include student work from is the end of semester reflection I assigned. Here is the assignment:

ENGL 1302 Reflection Assignment

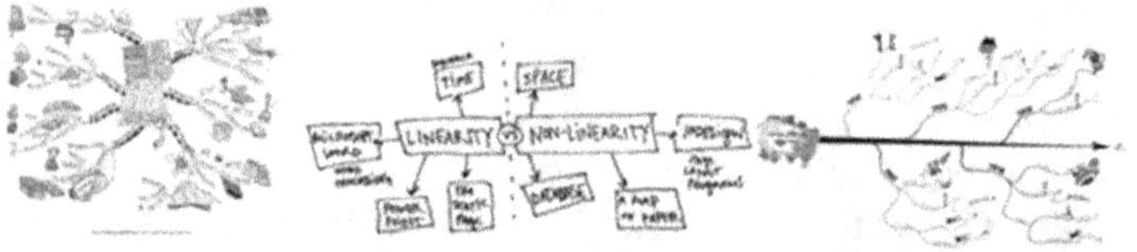

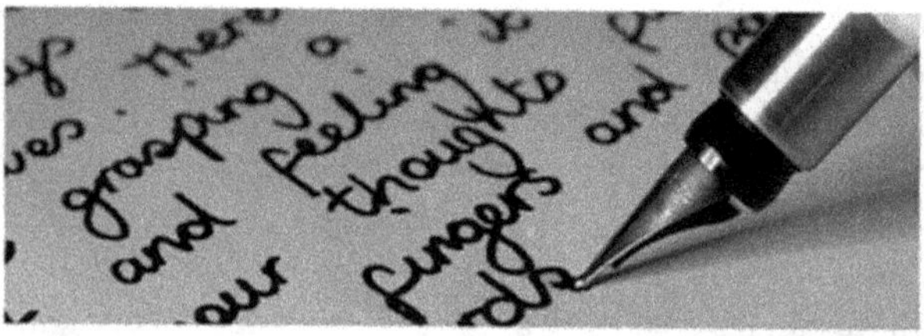

WHAT IS IT?
Your reflection is where you visually AND in writing tell a story of your journey through this class

PROMPT:

What/how/why have you learned in ENGL 1302 this semester?

TIPS /Guiding Questions
Use your reading reflections and drafts you have submitted on Blackboard to trace your work in this class.
What assignments did you enjoy? Why?
What assignments did you not enjoy? Why?
What readings impacted you? Why? How?
Have any of your opinions/understandings/processes changed over the course of this class? How? Why?
What perceptions of language/writing/reading/learning have been challenged or affirmed in this class? How? Why?
What have you learned in this class that you can apply to other classes/situations?

Figure 1.1 Writing Assignment.

These are some of the quotes that really stood out to me in terms of students being able to articulate their own identity affirmation in the writing classroom, questioning language, or their ability to transfer knowledge to new situations based on a specific translingual pedagogical tool I used in class.

Student 1

"When it comes to the most impactful reading that I was presented this semester, it would definitely have to be "Challenging our labels". I think this reading hits home when it comes to the entire ideology that this class presented this semester. The reason this reading impacted me is simply because it changed the way that I think for the most part, when it comes to the word "correct" the biggest thing that I received from this class was questioning what is presented to me. The biggest reason I enjoyed reading them was because they proposed a different view on writing that I didn't acknowledge before, some examples of this were "Sponsors of Literacy", "Codemeshing in Academic Writing: Identifying Teaching Strategies of Translanguaging", and a few more. The reason I enjoyed these the most was because they gave me more light on speaking two languages and things I knew about but never thought about. I had spent a lot of time reading these articles and definitely tried reflect what I learned. The greatest lessons I earned from this course were the meaning of Good Writing, the importance of drafts, translanguaging, and that it is okay to add your personal touch to writing. For most of us good writing had to be impeccable, without mistakes, but now I realize that good writing can be anything, it depends on the audience and purpose. Furthermore, this course gave me the opportunity to incorporate Spanish into my assignments (use translanguaging) and that made me feel very proud of my culture. My culture is a part of me, so essentially, I was adding my personal touch to my work. Nevertheless, I am no longer afraid to write drafts, because now I know that by writing them, I'll achieve a better final product."

Student 2

"For as long as I can remember, an "Intellectual" was a person who wrote, read, and spoke "White English,".... Canagarajah's reading impacted and changed my perception about writing by introducing codemeshing in my writing which is constructing knowledge from a different language or different methods of representation and using them in your writing. I am a Mexican-American girl who at times feels confused and torn between two worlds, The United States of America and Mexico. Although I have lived in the United States since birth, I lived in South Texas in a border city called Brownsville. Brownsville is the city that lies right next to the *Frontera* that separates the United States and Mexico. I am also a bilingual female who speaks both English and Spanish as I declare it as part of my identity. Before inquiring my 1302 English Rhetoric and Composition class, I was always scared to include Spanish phrases or words that enhance and connect with my writing, but after this semester, that fear no longer exists. My new understanding about writing or shall I say good writing, "Depends on whether it gets things done, and whether it accomplishes what the writer (and readers) need the writing to accomplish," and whether the writing represents the writer. My learnings in this class will not only benefit me in this course, but in any other course that involves writing. In the future, I hope to pursue a career as a dentist and throughout this course, it somehow gave me confidence to use my Spanish language without feeling ashamed about it."

Student 3

"I have changed my perspective on how I process my writing and reading because I feel I don't have a limit to how or what I can share. I really enjoyed learning about code meshing and translanguaging learning to combine my languages into this learning experience. Daily I use both my Spanish and English language I didn't want that to go to waste. However, translanguaging has help me understand how important it is to use it within your stories. Express our culture, *y estar orgullosa de poder tener y escibir en dos idiomas.*"

All three of these students not only found the idea of translingaluaging to be powerful, but explained how it resonated so deeply with them on an academic level and a personal level. I cannot imagine a space for these students that does not affirm their identity in this way.

Student 3, in particular, felt the need to include Spanish phrases in her reflection, showing that she felt confident in that language and actually demonstrating what she now understands to be good writing. She acknowledges that she doesn't want her daily use of both "Spanish and English" to "go to waste." Her profound analysis that if she doesn't use all of her language repertoire makes it a "waste" tells me that she has begun to shift how she feels about using all of her language capabilities as resources.

Similar to Student 3, Student 2 talks about her language use and how she sees her languages as beneficial in future situations. She talks about her future as a dentist and how the course "somehow gave [her] confidence to use [her] Spanish language without feeling ashamed about it." The thought that she had previously felt shame of a skill that she possesses but also of part of who she is harmful. The fact that she can now acknowledge her skills and feel pride in the idea of using them is positive.

Overall, these students reflected in their daily language use and what it means to them to see their language and resources rather than barriers. If translingual pedagogy had not been used, perhaps these realizations would not have been had.

Conclusions

Through these assignments, I noticed that my students were able to articulate on their own how certain translingual and culturally responsive pedagogical strategies positively impacted their identity, their belief in themselves, their confidence in their language use, their pride in their culture, how they will use language in other situations, and the way they see themselves as college students.

A few particular ideas that I have gleaned from this particular work is that engaging with multilingual and multicultural texts and identities affirms student linguistic abilities and identities, encouraging them to see themselves as scholars and researchers. Also, allowing/encouraging students to use the language that makes the most sense based on purpose and audience/allows them to make meaning. In addition, engaging with readings about code meshing/code switching/translanguaging allows students to explore and challenge language dominance, which they may have never been asked/told/allowed to do before. This can seriously encourage their own identity and use of language to be challenged or explored.

Obviously, my work is limited to my course, my section, my students, my pedagogy. Next steps include continuing to research HOW translingual and culturally relevant pedagogy impacts identity.

Works Cited

Alvarez, Steven. "Translanguaging Tareas: Emergent Bilingual Youth as Language Brokers for Homework in Immigrant Families." Language Arts. Vol. 91, no.5, 2014, pp. 326-339.

Canagarajah, Suresh. "Lingua Franca English, Multilingual Communities, and Language Acquisition." *The Modern Language Journal*, vol. 91, 2007, pp. 923-939 (2007).

—. *Translingual Practice: Global Englishes and Cosmopolitan Relations*. London/NewYork, Routledge, 2013.

García, Ofelia. "Translanguaging in Schools - Subiendo y Bajando, Bajando y Subiendo as Afterword." *Journal of Language, Identity & Education*, vol. 16, no. 4, 2017, pp. 256-263.

García, Ofelia., and Tatyana Kleyn, editors. *Translanguaging with Multilingual Students: Learning from Classroom Moments*. NewYork, Routledge, 2016.

Gilyard, Kieth. "The Rhetoric of Translingualism." *College English*, vol. 78, no.3, 2016, pp. 284-289.

Goldblatt, Eli. *Because We Live Here*. Hampton Press, 2007.

Horner, Bruce., et al. "Language Difference in writing: Toward a Translingual Approach." *College English*, vol. 73, no. 3, 2011, pp. 303-321.

Mignolo, Walter. *The Darker Side of the Renaissance: Literacy, Territoriality, and Colonization*. The University of Michigan Press, 2012.

Chapter 2

Translanguaging and Academic Writing: Possibilities and Challenges in English-Only Classrooms

Abu Saleh Mohammad Rafi and Professor Anne-Marie Morgan

James Cook University

Abstract: The study applied a translanguaging approach in a writing skill development class in the English department of a Bangladeshi public university. Data were collected through classroom observation, a pedagogical intervention, a focus group discussion with students, and a semi-structured interview with the class teacher. The study findings challenge monolingual approaches to academic writing in particular and demonstrate how a planned translanguaging approach allows teachers to relate English content to learners' local language(s) and experience, thus promoting greater understanding and metalinguistic awareness while also affirming the bilingualism and supporting bilingual learners in their classrooms. These findings have implications for policy and practices designed to improve learning outcomes, as well as to enhance the satisfaction and self-esteem of multilingual students studying in an otherwise monolingual classroom located in multilingual countries.

Keywords: translanguaging, academic writing, heteroglossia, English medium instruction, Bangladeshi university

***

Introduction

The potential benefits of using translanguaging pedagogies in writing instruction were investigated in the context of an English language course offered in a Bangladeshi public university. This university offers undergraduate and postgraduate degrees through its faculties and affiliated armed forces training institutes. Unlike other public universities in Bangladesh, this university provides education solely through the medium of English language from the first year in all disciplines. To prepare first-year students for English medium instruction, the Department of English provides a course entitled "Freshman English and Communication Skills Development." This course is designed to improve students' receptive and productive skills in "standard" English, across the domains of reading, writing, listening, and speaking, to the standard required to undertake courses at the tertiary level. These monoglossic and monolingual approaches to education focus solely on "correct" academic English language development since little to no use of home language practices, nor localized versions of English (used inside or outside the academy) are factored into classroom instruction (Wright and Baker).

Research on academic writing has demonstrated the challenges non-native students face writing academic English in international English-medium universities when their linguistic backgrounds differ from those of first language English speakers (Doyle, Motlhaka and Makalela). While translanguaging is defined as "the ability of multilingual speakers to shuttle between languages, treating the diverse languages that form their repertoires as an integrated system" (Canagarajah, "Codemeshing" 401) and has recently been explored as a pedagogical practice to differentiate and facilitate instruction for learners from diverse language backgrounds, enabling students to "cognitively engage with learning and to act on learning" (García and Wei 79), this study primarily examined how translanguaging could assist students in obtaining the required outcome in academic writing. The writing section of the course in focus covered product writing (in the specific genre), process writing (for a specific academic purpose), paragraph writing, essay writing, and summary writing. Data collected during a teaching about paragraph writing revealed possibilities for using translanguaging that could be transferred to other writing tasks.

The overall design of the study drew on a two-pronged ethnographic approach to investigate the following questions:

Research question 1: How does the ethnolinguistic ecology of the classroom provide scope for translanguaging in writing instruction?

Research question 2: What is the role of translanguaging in writing instruction in terms of facilitating academic writing?

Research question 3: Is translanguaging in writing instruction transferable across the curriculum?

As background to addressing these questions, translanguaging research and its intersection with writing are reviewed. The methodological approach used in the study is then presented, followed by the results and a discussion of implications for policy and practice in international higher education writing. While the focus of this study, like much of the literature, relates to English-medium instruction institutions, results are also useful for other multilingual higher education contexts. Importantly, research from the "periphery" (in contexts where English is not the dominant local language) provides needed insights into translanguaging practices in diverse contexts and speaks to implications for the resistance of the cultural hegemony of English-dominant nations in determining academic writing standards and approaches in higher education institutions.

Literature review

In the international higher education context, institutional policies often endorse assumptions based on the myth of linguistic and cultural uniformity (Gogolin). These policies rely on scripted curriculum and English-only language instruction divorced from the multilingual realities of students (Ascenzi-Moreno and Espinosa). Since multilingual students draw from multiple semiotic resources available to them, the language separation policy (i.e. the leaving of other semiotic resources at the classroom door) in literacy practices such as writing does not meet the students' needs in learning how to write in English as an additional language (L2). Even though L2 writing is strategically, rhetorically, and linguistically different from L1 writing, especially in higher education contexts, scholars argue that L1 writing simulates the conventions of L2 writing conventions since the L1 writers are often associated with judgments of lower writing quality despite the positive correlations between the presence of local cohesive devices and writing quality (Crossley et al.; Silva). With this in mind, scholars in academic writing have identified principles and practices for designing strategies that account for the diverse semiotic resources of students (Motlhaka and Makalela). A translanguaging pedagogical approach is one such strategy that promises to (at least partially) overcome the challenges in academic writing for linguistically and culturally diverse students (Busch; Canagarajah; García).

Translanguaging aids multilingual students in the writing process by supporting and scaffolding learning, expanding understanding, enhancing knowledge, solving problems, and developing metalinguistic awareness (García and Kano). Recent evidence suggests that students who use translanguaging strategies when writing academic English can access content to a greater extent and depth, and engage in critical thinking which is not (yet) possible- nor can be articulated- in the L2 instruction only classrooms (Ascenzi-Moreno and

Espinosa; García and Kleyn). Motlhaka and Makalela investigated how translanguaging provides optimal conditions for dialogic pedagogy for multilingual students to reflect on rhetorical conventions of both L1 and L2 writing and also the role of L1 in L2 writing. This capacity to compare and reflect on the different conventions is not usually attempted in L2-only teaching approaches, yet it allows for insights into both language systems that enhance and reinforce metalinguistic knowledge of benefit to all students in improving writing through increased knowledge of language conventions. Studies such as a three-year investigation by Adamson and Coulson demonstrated how the strategic use of translanguaging improved written work, facilitated the completion of tasks, resulted in improved outcomes for most students of lower proficiency, and enhanced authenticity and relevance to local purposes and positive perceptions of students toward a translanguaging policy (Adamson and Coulson). This, and like studies, therefore, indicate that translanguaging approaches ensure multilingual students are more successful in higher education, thus enhancing equity and inclusivity.

Beyond these educational benefits, translanguaging in writing is a means for a pragmatic approach to challenging linguistic inequality and inequity (Canagarajah). Because the colonial legacy and contemporary discourses of the devaluation of languages within the school, higher education, and broader society contribute to educational failure in terms of retaining students' heritage language competence over the course of schooling, these should be challenged (Cummins). Including translanguaging in the writing process teaching allows teachers to create a responsive environment where students can exhibit their agency as thinkers and writers, drawing on their own language practices while also focusing on English acquisition (Ascenzi-Moreno and Espinosa; Daniel and Pacheco). The close relationship between writing practices, the resources used for such practices and identity work (Lillis) are illustrated in a series of studies. Sebba et al. showed how the style, register, and language authors choose in writing contribute to the formation of their identities as writers. Motlhaka and Makalela found the use of L1 in L2 writing legitimizes L2 writers' multi-competent minds rather than artificially compartmentalizing two languages. Horner et al. argued that language varieties are resources to be sustained, capitalized on, and nurtured, encouraging educators to "confront the realities of language difference in writing in ways that honor and build on, rather than attempt to eradicate, those realities of difference in their work with their students" (313). Building on this perspective, Ascenzi-Moreno and Espinosa advocate for a focus in the classroom on "what writers do with language—what their purposes are and the reasons why—and not solely on whether the writer has written what is considered "standard" English" (12).

Resisting or transgressing established academic writing norms, however, can be costly since in most higher education institutions the teaching of writing has strict gate-keepers, and authors who use L1 resources may be treated as not proficient and penalized accordingly (Canagarajah; Sebba et al.). Hence, different approaches need to be considered in institutions where writing as a semiotic resource and practice is inscribed with identity(ies) (Lillis). Bakhtin's framework of heteroglossia is useful here to explain how socio-historical relationships give meaning to translanguaging approaches to writing pedagogy. Heteroglossia recognizes the different voices that are layered in a single text, including social, professional, dialectal, and jargon layers, all working against the pull of a unitary set of language norms (Kiramba). The constant struggle between heteroglossia and unitary language can be explained using Bakhtin's notions of centripetal (centralizing or unifying forces) and centrifugal (diversifying) forces (Kiramba; Lillis). Kiramba applied these notions to discuss the social tensions between policy and practice in multilingual writing practices:

> The centripetal forces may represent the language policies or assumptions on the part of teachers, parents, and communities that it is better to learn in one unitary language, while the centrifugal forces, such as translanguaging in writing, arise from the heteroglossia found in linguistically diverse classrooms (119).

Since the conventions of academic writing are not (or should not be) set in stone, Canagarajah argues that students can appropriate apparently unfavourable conventions and policies effectively to find their voice, with suitable negotiation strategies established by teachers. The assessment of academic writing, from this perspective, can be understood using translanguaging theory.

First, schools help to standardize particular lexical and structural features as acceptable in named languages such as English, Spanish, and Russian, whereas the use of language features by bilingual speakers goes beyond the bounded description of each language. Translanguaging helps teachers separate

> ... language-specific performances in the named language—English, Spanish, Russian, Chinese or others—from general linguistic performances, that is, the students' ability, for example, to argue a point, express inferences, communicate complex thoughts, use text-based evidence, tell a story, identify main ideas and relationships in complex texts, tell jokes, and so forth (García and Kleyn 24).

This argument points to the centrality of teachers in the learning process and in establishing and negotiating conditions for learning that recognizes these general L1 abilities, including in student writing. At the same time students are using translanguaging to learn the dominant language for social and educational purposes (Ascenzi-Moreno and Espinosa; Kiramba).

Given translanguaging has been shown to be beneficial in multilingual classrooms (Vertovec), and arguably all classrooms in a "superdiverse" world are multilingual, a translanguaging policy has the potential to empower Bangladeshi students by affirming their identity through their (pluri-)language use. In addition, by designing translanguaging into instruction, teachers can become actively involved in challenging language hierarchies and creating an interpersonal space that affirms participant identities and facilitates collaborative relations of power (Kiramba).

The Study

While the wider study covered eight Humanities and Social Sciences classrooms across four universities, this article specifically addresses data collected from the English department of a public university pseudonymized as the Ariya University of Excellence (AUE).

Participants and data collection

Two ethnographic methods were used to collect data. First, linguistic ethnography was used to undertake an observational study of the educational site (Copland and Creese) and, second, auto-ethnography was used to record a pedagogical intervention on paragraph organization (Hammersley and Atkinson). Altogether four sets of data were collected through classroom observations, pedagogical intervention, a student focus group discussion, and a semi-structured interview with the course tutor. The entire cohort of "ENG 1001: Freshman English and Communication Skills Development" students (approximately 57 students) and their course-instructor were observed during two different sessions. All participants in this study are Bangladeshi citizens with varying degrees of English language proficiency because they completed their pre-tertiary education in different streams, including Bangla medium and English medium instruction, and Madrassa (Islamic school) education.

The instructor Ms Shila (a pseudonym), a Bangladeshi national, completed her Bachelor's and Master's degree in the English department of a leading public university in Bangladesh. She is currently working as a lecturer while pursuing a Masters of Philosophy (MPhil) degree in code-switching. Alongside teaching and research, she looks for opportunities to pursue higher studies in English speaking countries. Although Ms Shila is yet to cross physical, cultural, linguistic and epistemological borders in the idyllic sense of transnationalism, her educational background and career plan revealed her transnational imaginaries of a deterritorialized space, "detached from local places and embedded in the imaginings of people" (Warriner 204). The discussion sections of this study described how Ms Shila affected her transnational process through cultivating education and literacy among her students in a global language while limiting the use of local language and culture in her class.

The intervention lesson on paragraph organization was designed using a translanguaging pedagogical approach. While the lesson was planned for the whole class, Ms Shila elected not to replace a full lesson with the intervention lesson conducted by us, as she was bound by institutional policy, and would have had to replace the intervention class with an additional class. Hence, a separate class was arranged with seven volunteer students, named (pseudonymously) Adiba, Nila, Jimmi, Tanjim, Shaki, Rakib, and Arka. Ms Shila also participated in the intervention class. A focus group discussion with the students was followed by the intervention lesson. Ms Shila was interviewed later. Observation and intervention data are de-identified to conform with the ethics approval protocols of the University of New England, Australia.

Data analysis

A thematic analysis of the data was undertaken using Bakhtin's notion of heteroglossia. Because the notion of heteroglossia accounts for all the voices in a text, it can be used to investigate the two conflicting pull of diversifying "centrifugal" and unifying "centripetal" forces in texts used in linguistically diverse classrooms. This notion was used to analyze the tension between policy and practice in the classroom where translanguaging pedagogy was used. The classroom observation data were analyzed through "versus coding"- a method of analysis in which the conflicts, struggles, and power issues are observed in social action, reaction, and interaction in dichotomous codes, such as, TEACHER VS. STUDENTS, TEACHER VS. POLICYMAKERS, BANGLA VS. ENGLISH, and so on (Saldaña). The pedagogical intervention produced two datasets: student-researcher interaction and student work samples. The combination of inductive and deductive reasoning was applied during the analysis to determine the impact of translanguaging pedagogy on writing styles (Uysal).

Participants mostly translanguaged during the focus group discussion and interview, using Bangla, English, and hybrid language utterances. We transcribed these two sets of data without translating all utterances into English. This decision was made to position translanguaging as a legitimate form of communication for multilingual participants and to acknowledge their "voice" which gives them the capacity to make themselves understood as situated subjects (Blommaert; García and Kleyn). A gloss of the discussion and interview was provided for supervisors without Bangla and x language knowledge. *In Vivo* coding was used to analyze the focus group and interview data since it entails coding based on the actual language used by the participants (Strauss and Corbin). Finally, we triangulated the focus group and interview data with observation data to generate broader themes for meta-analysis and conclusions.

Results and discussion

Ethnolinguistic ecology of the focal classroom

The analysis of the classroom observation revealed the monolingual ideology of the senior management enacted by teaching staff, and, to some extent, by the university students. The "English please" sign on the classroom walls illustrates the centripetal forces pulling towards an English-only environment (fig. 2.0).

Figure 2.0 "ENGLISH PLEASE" sign on the AUE classroom walls.

Typically, the welcome speech in this classroom is in English alongside a common Arabic greeting: "Salam". Arabic-English translanguaging has been normalized here as Bangladesh is a Muslim-majority country. However, the author felt that, despite understanding the intent of this study, Ms Shila was not comfortable with his translanguaged introduction in Bangla-English. On several occasions, Ms Shila discouraged students from translanguaging, when they elected to do so, and also discouraged the use of standard Bangla, even when it was used by students to clarify a point. For example, in the first observed class, when a student used Bangla to enquire about a specific rule on the correct use of prepositions, Ms Shila refused to answer, saying: "I will not tell you the rule unless you ask the question in English." On another occasion, a student used a Bangla translation "পুরাঘটিত" of present perfect/continuous tenses. Ms Shila adopted the practice of "pretending" not to understand that translation as a way of discouraging Bangla in the classroom; although later on, she continued using these Bangla terms "পুরাঘটিত" and "পুরাঘটিত চলমান" in a sarcastic way to explain perfect/continuous tenses. There were also instances in which Ms Shila asked a student to translate her response into English when the student spoke Bangla to explain why she changed her major from Economics to English. In this regulated linguistic environment, a student pointed out to Ms Shila that the English-only instruction, and the "English please" signpost, prevented students from freely expressing their ideas, as these occur naturally to them in one or other of their languages, and that they may not readily have the English to express these ideas under pressure in a classroom. Ms Shila responded, "If you practice English in classroom, you will speak English better when you go outside," highlighting the need for English language proficiency when studying abroad. That student reluctantly complied, hoping that he will be proficient in the English language upon completing this course. As soon as another student started speaking Bangla, his classmates shouted from the back: "English please." These cumulative efforts to impose one language over others are centripetal, to use Bakthinian terminology since they force speakers toward adopting a unified linguistic identity (Duranti). However, in this particular case, the motivation to obtain the mandatory English language proficiency was a more triggering factor than adopting a unified linguistic identity.

Regardless of the centripetal forces, awareness of and resistance to the unified approach were evident, as the classroom also featured centrifugal forces arising from the heteroglossia of translanguaging that included standardized Bangla use, as well as colloquial Bangla use, where slang words manifested interpersonal interaction among students to mock the standardized Bangla pronunciation used in official conversations between teacher and students. The students

often used informal registers with utterances such as "তুই এডা করছস ক্যান?" among themselves as a rapport-building tactic or "shit" to express frustrations over improperly printed question papers. In one instance, Ms Shila asked a student for confirmation in Bangla "বুঝতে পেরেছ?" (Understood?). As soon as the student hyper-corrected the pronunciation of "পেরেছি" ("yes, understood"), the whole class burst into laughter.

Figure 2.1 Student Observations.

The observation findings of this study diverge from studies where translanguaging was not viewed as a practice of deficiency (Canagarajah; Canagarajah; García) and where teachers and students use their linguistic resources as available, which may or may not challenge institutional policies (Kiramba). On the other hand, these findings converge with findings of studies where translanguaging is an unbidden product and occurs surreptitiously, and often behind the backs of teachers (Canagarajah; Heller and Martin-Jones; Martin-Beltrán).

The role of translanguaging in writing instruction

A standard paragraph is commonly represented in English as an additional language (EALD) teaching as comprising three major components: topic sentence, supporting details, and concluding sentence. Translanguaging instruction was designed to facilitate students' understanding of each of these components. We used translation, multilingual texts, and culturally relevant materials as scaffolds for explaining to students each component of the paragraph, and We invited cross-linguistic analysis for exploring writing conventions in English and Bangla. The following themes emerged from the analysis to demonstrate that translanguaging as used:

- as a scaffold and communicative norm;
- for cross-linguistic analysis;
- in writing conventions, and
- as identity performances.

Translanguaging as a scaffold and communicative norm in the classroom

The intervention lesson included a description of translanguaging theory in education and encouraged the participants to use all linguistic resources at their disposal. We also mentioned that these resources would be leveraged strategically as a tool to facilitate understanding of paragraph organization and to develop high order thinking skills while celebrating home languages and culture in the monocultural English department.

Because translanguaging means "the adoption of bilingual supportive scaffolding practices" (Doiz et al. 218) and translation can be one way to facilitate translanguaging (García and Kleyn), a Bangla definition of the topic sentence for the example paragraph was presented as a scaffold on PowerPoint slides. First, a student was asked to read it out for the class, and then another student was asked to summarise, in any language(s), what she understood from the definition. This second student used a little translanguaging, with mostly standard Bangla and a few interspersed English words to explain the topic sentence. Moreover, she used an example of a paragraph writing topic, a rainy day, to be more convincing. It is clear from her response that the deployment of translation as a translanguaging strategy provided students with access to the new content, i.e., the topic sentence. At this point, we provided the same definition in English and introduced some strategies on how to write a topic sentence. The two parts of a topic sentence, topic and controlling idea, were discussed. Following the same pattern, students read definitions of these concepts in Bangla, and then continued to translanguage in their discussion of what they understood. Finally, they read the same definitions in English. After the discussion, students were asked to complete a worksheet that required them to identify from examples the topic sentence and controlling ideas and to select the most effective topic sentence from three options.

We used the same strategy to lecture on supporting details and concluding sentences. Throughout the intervention, translanguaging occurred across a variety of language modes: reading, writing, listening, and speaking. This strategic manipulation of translanguaging differentiated instruction and made the all-English curriculum accessible for all students, allowing them to complete tasks effectively.

Cross-linguistic analysis

A translanguaged definition of transition words, along with few examples, was presented to the class. Transition words used as discourse markers help readers to make logical connections across different parts of written texts, and their presence or absence can directly affect the flow of reading (Motlhaka and Makalela). The frequency of transition words reveals differences in the rhetorical patterns of respondents' written work and signal the cultural impact of each writing style (Uysal). For this reason, we offered a cross-linguistic perspective on the transition words, by providing examples from British and Australian Englishes where transitional words such as "firstly," and "secondly" are used in an adverbial sense, unlike in American English, where these are used in an adjectival sense: "first" and "second." We asked the students which usage they preferred; the students immediately chose the adverbial use as Bangla also uses transition words in the adverbial sense. A student provided examples to explain: "'প্রথমত' বলি আমরা, 'প্রথম' বলি না" where the suffix "ত" in "প্রথমত" is an equivalent of "ly" in "firstly." The analysis of these data reveals a match between Bangla and British/Australian discourse conventions. In contrast, a study by Motlhaka and Makalela reported on the challenges Sesotho students encounter while making connections between ideas due to the mismatch between connective devices in Sesotho and English.

Upon further probing, the students also demonstrated awareness of a particular convention for using transition words such as অতএব, সুতরাং, প্রসঙ্গক্রমে, পরিশেষে to maintain coherence in academic writing, which tends to differ from their use in Bangla spoken discourse. Since writing experiences for the majority of bilingual students are often constrained and limited to isolated exercises solely in the new language (Fu), we disrupted those traditional practices by providing equivalent English transitional words for the Bangla examples the students brought to the class. This cross-linguistic analysis helped the students to understand English transitional words while brushing up Bangla ones too for academic writing purposes, increasing overall metalinguistic awareness.

Translanguaging in Writing conventions and identity performances

Since translanguaging offers two ways of understanding language use in assessment contexts (García and Kleyn), we were interested in gauging participant feelings towards this approach which was new for them. We provided a paragraph extracted from a Bangla newspaper article on the return of 1970s-style clothing for men in 2019 and engaged students in two writing tasks. The first task was designed to assess students' *general linguistic performances* in terms of understanding the paragraph organization, and the second task was to assess their *language-specific performances* in terms of writing an academic paragraph in English. The multilingual texts produced in the first task demonstrated how multilingual students represented their identities in English (Canagarajah). Surprisingly, only one student among seven took up the opportunity to translanguage in the first task (fig. 2.2).

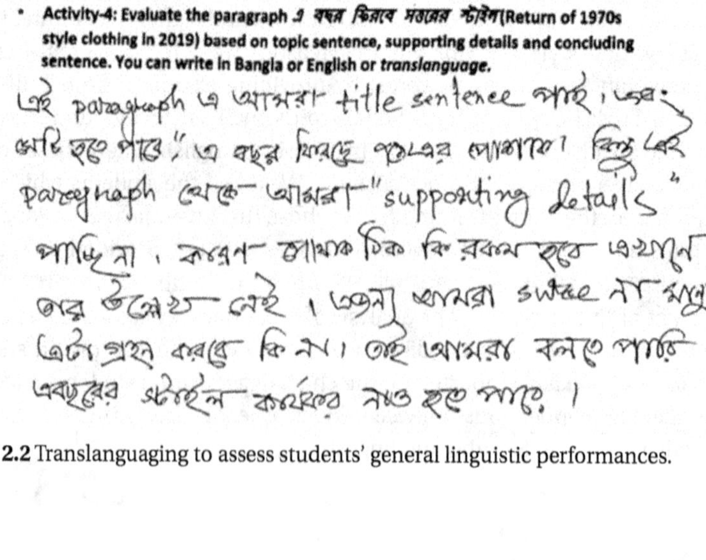

Figure 2.2 Translanguaging to assess students' general linguistic performances.

This student did not comment on the topic and concluding sentences and also confused the supporting details, providing information to the teacher on what further explanation was needed in subsequent lessons. Nonetheless, the text is an example of heteroglossia in practice, wherein the centripetal and centrifugal tensions of the utterances exist in a context where correctness is essential (Kiramba). The other six students, however, demonstrated a stronger understanding of paragraph organization and produced well-argued writing. For example, a student using English, except for the title of the article which was in Bangla, argued that the topic sentence is flawed in the sense that it mentioned 70s style in general but talked about men's clothing only (fig. 2.3).

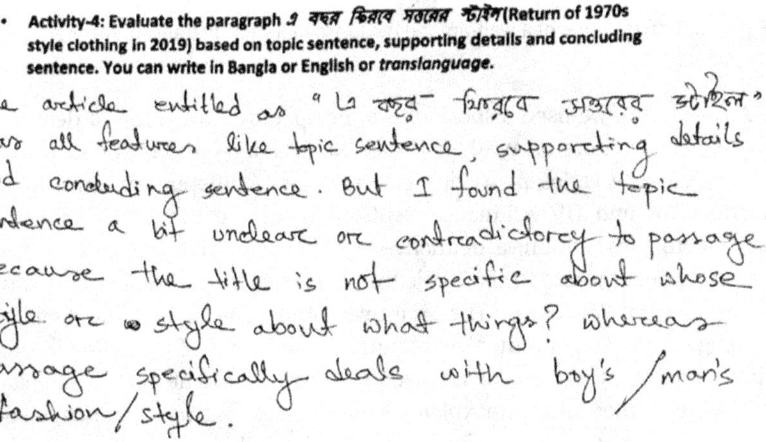

• **Activity-4: Evaluate the paragraph .৭ বছর কিরাব সতরের চীবণ(Return of 1970s style clothing in 2019) based on topic sentence, supporting details and concluding sentence. You can write in Bangla or English or *translanguage*.**

The article entitled as " ৭ বছর ফিরৱৈর সতরের চীবণ" has all features like topic sentence, supporting details and concluding sentence. But I found the topic sentence a bit unclear ore contradictorcy to passage. Because the title is not specific about whose style ore style about what things? whereas passage specifically deals with boy's /man's fashion/ style.

Figure 2.3 An example of a well-argued response in a slightly translanguaged script.

The third example demonstrated how the student critiqued the placement of the topic sentence in the paragraph, which might not be appropriate for elementary readers. This student also comments on the ineffectiveness of the concluding sentence (fig. 2.4).

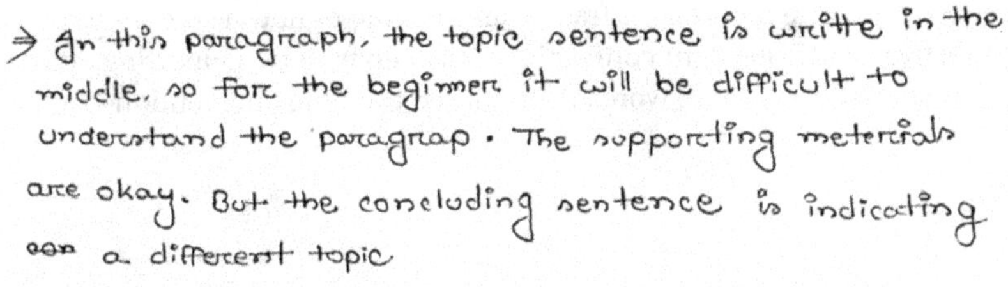

→ In this paragraph, the topic sentence is writte in the middle, so fore the beginner it will be difficult to understand the paragrap. The supporting meterials are okay. But the concluding sentence is indicating a different topic

Figure 2.4 An example of a well-argued response in an English script.

In the fourth example, the student argued that regardless of an unclear topic sentence or lack of supporting details, this paragraph has successfully conveyed the message to its readers (fig. 2.5).

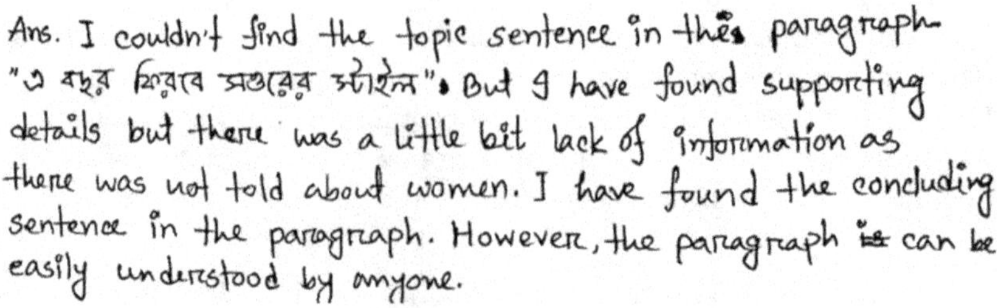

Ans. I couldn't find the topic sentence in this paragraph. "৩ বছর কিয়াব সত্তরের স্টাইল". But I have found supporting details but there was a little bit lack of information as there was not told about women. I have found the concluding sentence in the paragraph. However, the paragraph is can be easily understood by anyone.

Figure 2.5 An example of a well-argued response in a slightly translanguaged script.

At this point, we used a sociocultural perspective on writing to demonstrate the effect of culture on writing (Uysal). Kubota argued that the inductive and deductive style varies in writing conventions of different cultures. In essay-writing, UK and US writing conventions place the thesis statement in the introductory paragraph, a deductive style of writing. In contrast, in Sesotho writers wait to the end to clarify the thesis, an inductive style of writing (Kubota; Motlhaka and Makalela). The examples above reveal that the Bangladeshi writing convention is inductive, requiring a high level of reasoning in order to draw inferences and make connections external to the text. Motlhaka and Makalela argued that unexplained differences between language-specific conventions potentially result in confusion and disaffirmation of identity positions of students from diverse linguistic backgrounds.

In the assessment task that followed, students were asked to write using a deductive style: "What do you think about the return of 1970s clothing style in 2019? Write a paragraph in English explaining your reasons."

The deductive style was emphasized since the university considers this style appropriate for academic writing. All students came up with fully-fledged paragraphs which included all components and deductive writing style conventions. The following extract is an example of how a student wrote in a deductive style using tight connections between various supporting details by drawing on the transition words they learned from the intervention (fig. 2.6).

a paragraph in English explaining your reasons.

My opinion about the return of 1970's clothing
style in 2019

I think the return of 1970's clothing style in 2019 will
bring a traditional effect in our fashion. As, we are the
                                    Firstly
new generation and we do not have any idea about the
1970's clothing style properly, this year in 2019 the return
of 1970's clothing style will give us an style idea of that
era. But from some sources we come to know that the
      Secondly,
style in 1970 was to make clothes by tailoring. So, the
clothes will be attractive and according to own choice.
& Finally, I hope that in 2019 the return of 1970's clothing
style in 2019 will bring a change in our fashion and
culture.

Figure 2.6 An example of language specific performance of translanguaging pedagogy.

The writing task using translanguaging that preceded this assessment task helped students understand the lecture, organize their ideas in the assessment, and produce a final product. A student explained that the first task helped them attempt the second one since it served as a plan for writing the final product. They wrote "openly" without any language barrier in the first task and then "translated" their thoughts in the second one. This is how the strategic approach to assessing students' performance captured an accurate picture of their understanding of the topic. Although the student said that he "translated" what he understood in the first task, "translation" is the wrong word here since the second task was different, and the students transferred their newly gained knowledge creatively in the second task. The manipulation of authentic material in the writing task enhanced students' sociolinguistic awareness. The students felt "more dignified," and "proud'" to read material on Bangladeshi fashion in this English-only classroom and to promote their culture through writing in an international language like English. This finding can be interpreted using the Sebba et al. terminology of "envoicing" through which multilingual students can deviate from homogeneous uses and collective language norms to personalize their identity and voice.

Participant responses to the translanguaging classroom

Translanguaging as the medium of instruction

The pedagogical intervention allowed the students to look closely at their linguistic practices and question the traditional ways languages have been perceived. Their responses provided insights into how their identities and language resources could be recognized. The student Shaki, for example, drew on the fact that Bangla language has already embraced numerous features from different "named" languages in the course of its sub-continental history. With this in mind, Nila wondered why people are so strongly against mixing features of English with Bangla in the academic context while having no reservation about mixing features from Urdu, Arabic, and other named languages. Overall, the students felt that the ambiguous ideology against Bangla-English translanguaging in education does not align with the linguistic realities of their lives, and it silences their authentic voices, a view also articulated by Kiramba. Students appreciated translanguaging pedagogy since it disrupted the artificial monoculture and created an authentic space for plurilingual students and activated their (minimally) bilingual ways of learning. The student Shaki explained:

> In today's class, use of translanguaging was good because we usually talk in translanguaging outside, in our home, or with our friends. So whenever we use translanguaging in teaching or learning, and we can catch the information easily as usually, we talk like this.

Ms Shila, despite the requirement for her to conform to institutional requirements and directions, found the translanguaging class very useful in terms of improving the higher-level engagement of students and promoting more in-depth learning. The English only environment affects the students' motivation to concentrate on the lecture, and Ms Shila often has to negotiate with the school policy to hold their attention in the regular classroom. She said:

> Actually, when we speak in English for an hour and 30 minutes in the classroom without using any Bengali (aka Bangla in the nativized form), I find when students feeling sleepy and sometimes just losing their attention, not being able to get the meaning and most of the time I do use Bengali as a kind of icebreaker. When I find them feeling sleepy, I start speaking in Bengali.

An English only classroom also adds extra layers of complexity and affects the spontaneous participation of the students. Ms Shila sheds light on the struggle both teachers and students encounter to explain and understand

English language and literature content which is alien to Bangladeshi culture. From her observation, the strategic use of translanguaging facilitated students' understanding of paragraph organization, including in Bangla texts, and drawing their attention to language conventions that differ between languages and cultures. She adds that although she always feels the necessity for switching between languages to contextualize the content, she cannot do so due to the strict implementation of the English-only policy. To this end, Ms Shila concludes by saying: "the medium of instruction should not be confined only on a language that is not your native tongue."

Translanguaging in writing and assessment

The participants provided varied responses to translanguaging in writing tasks. The students acknowledged the benefits of assessing general linguistic performance for increasing their overall understanding of both languages and academic writing needs. The student Shaki recommended incorporating this type of assessment or worksheet in each class so that teachers understand if students can apply new knowledge acquired from the lecture of that day. There are regular instances when teachers reluctantly, but pragmatically switch to Bangla, "transgressing" the English-only policy to make students understand a new topic or to elicit a response. Under such circumstances, Rakib found that assessing students' general linguistic performance suits the linguistic ecology of the classroom. Everybody agreed with him confirming: "এটা আসলে ১০০% যুক্তিযুক্ত বলা যায়" (It can be said, it is 100% logical to assess students this way). In light of this discussion, Tanjim shared how forgetting an English expression affected her exam-success, although she could answer that question, about English language poetry forms, in Bangla.

আমাদের first যে exam টা ছিল Introduction to Poetry সেখানে poetic কিছু name দেয়া ছিল ওগুলার explanation দিতে হবে, সেখানে আমার complete বাংলাটা মনে আছে, কিন্তু বাংলাটার মধ্যে কিছু কিছু English আছে, সেগুলো আমার মনে নাই। আমি শব্দটা change করতে পারবনা, ওইটার alternative নিয়েও আসতে পারব না। সে জন্য total টাই আমার ওখানে কাটা গেছে। (We were required to explain few literary terminologies in our first exam of *Introduction to Poetry* course. I can write the Bangla definition entirely, but I'd to write in English… there are few English terminologies that I cannot change, nor can I use some alternative words… so I have to give up the complete section).

Figure 2.7 Student Reflection.

Mbirimi-Hungwe argues that creating linguistic boundaries in a multilingual individual is a futile exercise since multilingual students like Tanjim in our study possess linguistic repertoires from which they draw when the need arises (García and Wei). Under those circumstances, a provision to translanguage in writing assessment can transgress the monolingual norm and reflect students' struggle to appropriate legitimized vocabulary items in their writing, while at the same time communicating their realities and providing comprehensible answers (Kiramba).

Regardless of the missed opportunities, several students argued in favor of monolingual or language-specific assessment for practical reasons, or potentially for fear of "slippage" in English use, which would not serve their broader learning purposes (i.e. buying into the "English please" instruction, based on it being for students' own good and the only way to improve English use). Jimmi argued that the assessor might not like the way students mix language features in an exam script, hence writing only in English or Bangla will keep them on the safe side. This argument rightly identifies the agency and discretion of teachers/markers in negotiating acceptable language use, and this may not always favour students' language choices, no matter how much more they could demonstrate with translanguaged responses. Ms Shila's ideologies about monolingual assessment, conditioned by the university policy, validate Jimmi's argument, as she said,

> "If the medium of instruction says that all the things should be taught in English then the assessment system should be only on that particular language, I mean if my focus is teaching English only, then I should assess them in English."

These responses reveal the tension-filled process of translanguaging in writing in contexts where emerging alternatives are still embryonic. Kiramba highlights the tensions multilingual writers go through in the process of finding a balance between authorial intentions and the authoritarian single-voicedness required by the school. As can be seen, the centripetal forces are in this instance currently stronger here than centrifugal ones, which also encouraged students to adopt the voice of the authority and assume their own agency in language determination (Bakhtin; Motlhaka and Makalela). Furthermore, the Bangladeshi education system is extremely competitive by nature due to the country's limited resources, and opportunities to study abroad in English speaking nations remain a highly desirable goal for young people and their parents. Hence, it was the student Rakib's perspective that assessing general linguistic performance will do injustice to those high-achieving students who worked hard to master the language since this "alternative" type of assessment will favour the students who lack proficiency in the target language. This particular finding contrasts with the studies that claimed translanguaging as a vehicle towards social justice for its potential to nullify the "standard language ideology" within the context of critical multicultural stories and real classroom situations (García-Mateus and Palmer; Ndlhovu).

Implications for policy and practices

The study reported here has several implications for policy and practices in the English departments of Bangladeshi universities. A combination of findings provides strong support for the conceptual premise that a translanguaging policy can offer space to voices that have been silenced in the artificial monoculture of the English department (García and Flores; Kiramba). However, the results are not yet fully encouraging in terms of incorporating translanguaging in academic writing practices in these institutions. Multilingual writing can be accommodated in classroom practices, but in terms of implementing it into assessment, Ms Shila thinks that the entire assessment system has to be revised, and is currently far from accepting alternative approaches both to the kinds of assessment and how it is implemented. She argues:

> "The current system completely depends on memorizing something. Some students try to memorize [even no matter] even they are good in English or Bengali or not, but they try to memorize and produce those in the exam script."

In this regard, translanguaging can be a valuable meaning-making process since it provides a space for creativity and criticality, whereby multilingual individuals can not only communicate ideas but also make identity representations for themselves (Wei). Nonetheless, translanguaging practices do not guarantee success, considering the views that prevail in these institutions about what is good academic writing (Canagarajah). Many teachers might not want to adopt translanguaging practices, even when they are aware of its benefits for students, fearing that the general community and institutional authorities will not understand the use of strategic manipulation and accommodation of authentic linguistic repertoires. Despite a renovated institutional policy, teachers might still face criticism and prejudice if the ethnolinguistic environment of the workplace is more accurately represented and reflected in programs. Ms Shila explained:

> Then again in the context of Bangladesh, we're very doubtful of others, so দেখা যাচ্ছে যে when a teacher is using Bengali, for example when it's written English in the university, then definitely they will be sceptical

about my proficiency, and they will think that the teacher is not good at English, that's why she is using Bengali.

Under those circumstances, teacher education programs and enhancing the prestige of translanguaging practices are fundamental requirements for implementing translanguaging as a pedagogical approach in higher education (García and Kleyn; Mazak and Carroll). The policymakers and educators must agree on the use of multilingual resources as legitimate cognitive tools and resources for communication in educational contexts to allow authentic voices and inclusive instruction (Kiramba).

The next challenge to overcome is to determine when and where translanguaging should be used, and how popular opinion might be influenced by international evidence. Ms Shila recommends:

আমার মনে হয় for the students of first year যেটা আমি মনে করেছিলাম, প্রথমে explain it in English, explain it in Bengali then translate in English. Gradually when they will be students of the second year or third year, আসতে আস্তে মনে হয় এই level টাকে কমিয়ে নিয়ে আসা উচিত By that time, they will be used to this language, and for the students of the fourth year or MA, only context-specific things, Bengali or their native language-- whatever they have can be used there only.

Figure 2.8 Ms Shila's Recommendation.

In other words, Ms Shila suggested using translanguaging was valid from an epistemological orientation and recommended adaptations based on learners' needs. This recommendation is feasible since translanguaging has been proven effective in terms of providing epistemic access to students and facilitating a more in-depth understanding of the content, biliteracy development and identity formation in complex multilingual spaces (Makalela). Further changes will take time, and the dissemination of and inclusion of more teachers and students in ongoiong research.

Conclusion

In answer to the first research question on the linguistic ecology of the classroom, the focal classroom viewed translanguaging as an unbidden product and a practice of deficiency. The observation findings contrast with the existing translanguaging literature since the participants gained little to no benefit from using their linguistic resources to confront entrenched institutional policies. Instead, institutional authorities, including some current teachers and students, made cumulative efforts to impose the English language over their authentic linguistic practices. This claim is also evident where six out of seven student participants did not avail themselves of the opportunity to translanguage in the first writing task discussed above.

In answer to the second question on the role of translanguaging in writing instruction, the findings in the pedagogical intervention where translanguaging differentiated instruction was used are consistent with the literature, demonstrably making the all-English curriculum accessible for all students. The translanguaged writing practice transformed traditional exercises that are limited solely to the target language. It also opened up possibilities for cross-linguistic analysis and a more in-depth understanding of rhetorical language conventions across cultures. The manipulation of authentic materials in a writing task tapped into students' sociolinguistic awareness, enhanced self-esteem, and affirmed their identity positions. All these findings were confirmed in the focus group discussions, as well as in the intervention lesson.

In answer to the third question on the transferability of translanguaging across the curriculum, it seems that, at this stage in this university, translanguaging can be suitable for providing only the epistemic access in classroom practices if not in assessment since the centripetal tensions of English-only ideology are stable and entrenched in the context. Regardless, this study provides valuable insights in terms of incorporating translanguaging into policy, to enact change based on evidence, given that very few studies have so far dealt with translanguaging in writing, and further studies could explore the benefits in different cohorts and with different writing tasks. Most of the extant studies are product-oriented (i.e., textual interpretation), and few are about discourse strategies (Canagarajah). Since this study has gone some way towards enhancing our understanding of both areas, further research should be undertaken to enhance the prestige of translanguaging practices so that educators can take translanguaging as one of a suite of pedagogic tools to create affirmative writing spaces, and to pass on their findings to the policy level for enhancing multilingual students' authentic engagement in writing.

Works Cited

Adamson, John., and David Coulson. "Translanguaging in English Academic Writing Preparation." *International Journal of Pedagogies and Learning*, vol. 10, no. 1, 2015, pp. 24-37.

Ascenzi-Moreno, Laura., and Cecilia M. Espinosa. "Opening up Spaces for Their Whole Selves: A Case Study Group's Exploration of Translanguaging Practices in Writing." *NYS Tesol Journal*, vol. 5, no. 1, 2018, pp. 10-29.

Bakhtin, Mikhail M. "Questions of Literature and Aesthetics." *Moscow: Fiction*, vol. 2, 1975.

Blommaert, Jan. "Bourdieu the Ethnographer: The Ethnographic Grounding of Habitus and Voice." *The Translator*, vol. 11, no. 2, 2005, pp. 219-236.

Busch, Brigitta. "Building on Heteroglossia and Heterogeneity: The Experience of a Multilingual Classroom." *Heteroglossia as Practice and Pedagogy*, Springer, 2014, pp. 21-40.

Canagarajah, Suresh. *Writing as Translingual Practice in Academic Contexts.* Taylor & Francis, 2013.

—. "Codemeshing in Academic Writing: Identifying Teachable Strategies of Translanguaging." *The Modern Language Journal*, vol. 95, no. 3, 2011, pp. 401-417.

—. "Moving out of the Monolingual Comfort Zone and into the Multilingual World: An Exercise for the Writing Classroom." *Literacy as Translingual Practice*, Routledge, 2013, pp. 215-222.

Copland, Fiona., and Angela Creese. *Linguistic Ethnography: Collecting, Analysing and Presenting Data.* Sage, 2015.

Crossley, Scott A., et al. "The development and use of cohesive devices in L2 writing and their relations to judgments of essay quality." *Journal of Second Language Writing*, vol. 32, 2016, pp. 1-16.

Cummins, Jim. "A Proposal for Action: Strategies for Recognizing Heritage Language Competence as a Learning Resource within the Mainstream Classroom." *Modern Language Journal*, vol. 89, no.4, 2005, pp. 585-592.

Daniel, Shannon M., and Mark B Pacheco. "Translanguaging Practices and Perspectives of Four Multilingual Teens." *Journal of Adolescent & Adult Literacy*, vol. 59, no. 6, 2016, pp. 653-663.

Doiz, Aintzane., et al. "Globalisation, Internationalisation, Multilingualism and Linguistic Strains in Higher Education." *Studies in higher education*, vol. 38, no. 9, 2013, pp. 1407-1421.

Doyle, Howard. "Multi-Competence, ELF, Learning and Literacy: A Reconsideration." *International Journal of Social Science and Humanity*, vol. 5, no. 10, 2015, p. 887.

Duranti, Alessandro. "Agency in Language." *A companion to linguistic anthropology*, 2004, pp. 451-473.

Fu, Danling. *Writing between Languages: How English Language Learners Make the Transition to Fluency, Grades 4-12*. Heinemann Portsmouth, NH, 2009.

García, Ofelia. "Emergent Bilinguals and Tesol: What's in a Name?" *TESOL Quarterly*, vol. 43, no. 2, 2009, pp. 322-326.

García, Ofelia., and Naomi Kano. "Translanguaging as Process and Pedagogy: Developing the English Writing of Japanese Students in the Us." *The multilingual turn in languages education: Opportunities and challenges*, 2014, pp. 258-277.

García, Ofelia., and Nelson Flores. "Multilingualism and Common Core State Standards in the United States." *The Multilingual Turn*, Routledge, 2013, pp. 157-176.

García, Ofelia., and Tatyana Kleyn, editors. *Translanguaging with multilingual students: Learning from classroom moments*. Routledge, 2016.

García, Ofelia., and Li Wei. "Translanguaging and Education." *Translanguaging: Language, Bilingualism and Education*, Springer, 2014, pp. 63-77.

García-Mateus, Suzanne., and Deborah Palmer. "Translanguaging Pedagogies for Positive Identities in Two-Way Dual Language Bilingual Education." *Journal of Language, Identity & Education*, vol. 16, no. 4, 2017, pp. 245-255.

Gogolin, Ingrid. "Linguistic and Cultural Diversity in Europe: A Challenge for Educational Research and Practice." *European Educational Research Journal*, vol. 1, no. 1, 2002, pp. 123-138.

Hammersley, Martyn., and Paul Atkinson. *Ethnography: Principles in Practice.* Routledge, 2007.

Heller, Monica., and Marilyn Martin-Jones. *Voices of Authority: Education and Linguistic Difference.* vol. 1, Greenwood Publishing Group, 2001.

Horner, Bruce., et al. "Language Difference in Writing: Toward a Translingual Approach." *College English*, vol. 73, no. 3, 2011, pp. 303-321.

Kiramba, Lydiah Kananu. "Translanguaging in the Writing of Emergent Multilinguals." *International Multilingual Research Journal*, vol. 11, no. 2, 2017, pp. 115-130.

Kubota, Ryuko. "An Investigation of L1–L2 Transfer in Writing among Japanese University Students: Implications for Contrastive Rhetoric." *Journal of Second Language Writing*, vol. 7, no. 1, 1998, pp. 69-100.

Lillis, Theresa. *Sociolinguistics of Writing.* Edinburgh University Press, 2013.

Makalela, Leketi. "Translanguaging as a Vehicle for Epistemic Access: Cases for Reading Comprehension and Multilingual Interactions." *Per Linguam: a Journal of Language Learning=Per Linguam: Tydskrif vir Taalaanleer*, vol. 31, no. 1, 2015, pp. 15-29.

Martin-Beltrán, Melinda. "The Two-Way Language Bridge: Co-constructing Bilingual Language Learning Opportunities." *The Modern Language Journal*, vol. 94, no.2, 2010, pp. 254-277.

Mazak, Catherine M., and Kevin S. Carroll, editors. *Translanguaging in Higher Education: Beyond Monolingual Ideologies.* Multilingual Matters, 2016.

Mbirimi-Hungwe, Vimbai. "Stepping Beyond Linguistic Boundaries in Multilingual Science Education: Lecturer's Perceptions of the Use of Translanguaging." *Southern African Linguistics and Applied Language Studies*, 2019, pp. 1-12.

Motlhaka, Hlaviso A., and Leketi Makalela. "Translanguaging in an Academic Writing Class: Implications for a Dialogic Pedagogy." *Southern African Linguistics and Applied Language Studies*, vol. 34, no. 3, 2016, pp. 251-260.

Ndlhovu, F. "Language, Migration, Diaspora: Challenging the Big Battalions of Groupism." *The Oxford handbook of language and society*, 2017, pp. 141-160.

Saldaña, Johnny. *The Coding Manual for Qualitative Researchers.* Sage, 2015.

Sebba, Mark., et al. *Language Mixing and Code-Switching in Writing: Approaches to Mixed-Language Written Discourse.* Routledge, 2012.

Silva, Tony. "Toward an Understanding of the Distinct Nature of L2 Writing: The ESL Research and Its Implications." *TESOL Quarterly*, vol. 27, no. 4, 1993, pp. 657-677.

Strauss, Anselm., and Juliet Corbin. *Basics of Qualitative Research Techniques.* Sage publications, Thousand Oaks, CA, 1998.

Uysal, Hacer Hande. "Tracing the Culture Behind Writing: Rhetorical Patterns and Bidirectional Transfer in L1 and L2 Essays of Turkish Writers in Relation to Educational Context." *Journal of Second Language Writing*, vol. 17, no. 3, 2008, pp. 183-207.

Vertovec, Steven. "Towards Post-Multiculturalism? Changing Communities, Conditions and Contexts of Diversity." *International social science journal*, vol. 61, no. 199, 2010, pp. 83-95.

Warriner, Doris S. "Transnational Literacies: Immigration, Language Learning, and Identity." *Linguistics and Education*, vol. 18, 2007, pp. 204.

Wei, Li. "Moment Analysis and Translanguaging Space: Discursive Construction of Identities by Multilingual Chinese Youth in Britain." *Journal of Pragmatics*, vol. 43, no. 5, 2011, pp. 1222-1235.

Wright, Wayne E., and Colin Baker. "Key Concepts in Bilingual Education." *Bilingual and Multilingual Education*, 2017, pp. 65–79.

Chapter 3

Language, Home, and Transnational Space

Naoko Akai-Dennis, PhD

Bunker Hill Community College

Abstract: It seems that there is an unwarranted assumption that a term with the prefix 'trans" brings something new and therefore beneficial, because the prefix implies that we go beyond something confining. In the same logical vein, transnational spaces might be unwarrantedly considered as advantageous to multi-linguals since the prefix "trans" could help destabilize linguistic boundaries. To reimagine social spaces for translingual practices in first-year writing classrooms, this article starts with an examination of different ideas of transnational space in other disciplines. This examination involves inquiries into different notions of nation and their associated notions of language, leading to Suresh Canagarajah's and Alastair Pennycook's theoretical endeavors to dismantle the notion of language as a pre-coded system in order to make translingual practices rigorous. These revisits of the taken-for-granted notions of nation and language vitalize the question of whether a transnational space is a precondition for translingual practices or a result of the practices. This questioning is enabled by ethnographic inquiries into not only the author's first-year writing classrooms and her students' languaging but also their social spaces outside of the classroom and their languaging there. Drawing on Derrida's concepts of monolingualism and relation between language and self as "inalienable alienation," the author argues that this fluid relation sometimes enables and other times disenables speakers to exert their agencies over languages in respective social spaces. The author further argues that the exertion of their linguistic agencies hinges on power relations in social spaces where different cultures, languages, and ideologies clash, and thus transnational space is not a precondition but a result of translingual practices. The article ends with a provocative statement that leads teachers in the first-year writing courses to ponder on.

Keywords: contact zones, monolingualism, transnational space, translingual practices, power imbalance, first-year writing, languaging, nation and language, social spaces

***

Rapid flows of people, information, languages, cultures, and commodities across geographical borders among nations could destabilize static concepts of nation, identity, language, and belonging. Along with this digital and physical transnational flow, some scholars have attempted to theoretically dismantle some borders among languages, nations, etc., which confine and immobilize some people within the borders. Over thirty years ago, for example, Martin and Mohanty already argued that situated notions of nation, community, and home are not only constructed but simultaneously contain and reconstruct effects of "a constant re-conceptualization of the relationship between personal and group history and political priorities" (210). Or some other scholars have attempted to strategize ways to cross borders, without destabilize them (Anzaldúa; Beverley; Giroux; Grewal; Pathak). Despite these efforts and on-going transnational flows, some borders or walls still exist or are even reinforced.

One of the divisive walls exists both between languages and within a language. This wall might not have been even recognized as a "wall," but rather has been successfully used to keep the integrity or purity of language. This successful use of linguistic walls, further, designates "dialects" or other versions of the language "derivative" (McWhorter). This linguistic wall is culturally, historically, socially, and even racially constructed and still rampant in not only English classrooms but also the academic fields. May in *The Multilingual Turn* explains that monolingualism has permeated so deeply in SLA and TESOL that both fields are rooted in the belief that learning a language is a "hermetic process uncontaminated by knowledge and use of one's other language" (2).

First-Year Writing classrooms are not always free from this invisible wall, which will come in different shapes and forms, since some writing classes seem to have been chronically haunted with linguistic homogeneity, or monolingualism (Kachru; Lyiscott; Pennycook; Young). They have nurtured the prevalent and dominating linguistic ideology by disseminating certain ways of expressing thoughts, emotions, opinions, etc. in the pretense that they teach the "proper" use of language as legitimate knowledge to first-year college students. In 1974, the Conference on College Composition and Communication declared a resolution upholding "Students' Right to Their

Own Language." However, these rights have been denied in many writing courses by the ideology of monolingualism.

Given this long-standing history of linguistic homogeneity in first-year writing classrooms, it is imperative to inquire into the theoretical underpinnings for the notion of language in order to disrupt linguistic homogeneity in writing classrooms and beyond. This inquiry is also necessary for one of the purposes of this book, the evaluation of ways to create transnational spaces in which translingual pedagogy or curriculum is implemented. That is because the quality and nature of transnational spaces depend on how language is conceptualized in the theories of translingual(ism)[1]. If translingual(ism) derives from the same concept of language that has sustained linguistic homogeneity, translingual pedagogy is not, and will not be, so promising as the prefix "trans" could imply. If translingual practices and/or translanguaging is rooted in the same concept of language that feeds into privilege of some students, transnational spaces in which translingual pedagogy is implemented do not benefit multilingual students. As Martin and Mohanty demonstrate in their endeavor, it is the vital "constant re-conceptualization" of language, nation, and belonging that I hinge on in order to inquire into social spaces where people perform translanguaging or any other form of translingual practice and (im)possibility of constructing transnational spaces in first-year writing classrooms.

Before I begin with an inquiry into notions of language, I am going to start by examining different concepts of "transnational spaces" in some disciplines. Understandably, the idea of transnational spaces is not discussed and refined in the academic disciplines that have supported and embraced the trendy translingual pedagogy. It seems that there is an unwarranted assumption that transnational spaces are "good" because "trans" implies that we go beyond something, or transnational spaces are beneficial, presumably, to multiple language users who can perform translingual practices since "trans" implies that linguistic homogeneity can be dismantled. Instead of entrusting this assumption, it is paramount to examine different ideas of transnational spaces in other disciplines because it allows me to reimagine social spaces for translingual pedagogy.

---

[1] I insert "ism" in a parenthesis because "ism" is dogmatic, while translingual practice, translingual approach, and other tranlingual pedagogies do not provide us with dogma. But I want to use this term to capture a wider range of ideas about this new concept.

Transnational Space

To describe places where people from different nations, cultures, customs, beliefs, and languages meet, scholars have used various terms such as transnational space, transnational community, multilingual community, diaspora, etc. The disciplinary fields such as area studies, cultural studies, sociology, recently embrace the notion of "space" because this term connotes unbound-ness and fluidity. Delineating differences between diaspora and transnational spaces, Faist, a sociologist, discusses that transnational(ism) is more embedded in "geographic and sociological images such as 'space' and 'field'" (16). Likewise, transnational social spaces implicate mobility and fluidity more than the concept of transnational community because transnational community could inscribe "neatly separate community narratives" (Hemphill and Blakely 79). Sheringham, a cultural geographer, discusses that transnational spaces are not only multidimensional and heterogeneous but also are increasingly porous (63). Those spaces will be less rigid and oppressive for multilinguals. This fluidity in transnational spaces will enable multilinguals to deploy any linguistic resources and repertoire available to them.

On the other hand, some scholars conceptualize transnational spaces in a quite different way. From transnational migration studies, Dahinden describes transnationality as "an alternative to integration or as the condition of being 'integrated' in the host country" (70). Shiller, a social anthropologist, points out that the current trend to essentialized national identity is manifested within the research of transnational community. A transnational space is simply considered by some camps of scholars to comprise different people from different nations, thereby fortifying those differences as opposed to the sameness.

These different conceptions of "transnational" can be ascribed to the different notions of nation. Nations have been assumed as static places which are reified by national state borders. However, this notion has been revisited and reconceptualized from different theoretical perspectives. From postcolonial feminist perspectives, Mohanty questions the static notion of nation, pointing out that the notion of nation has been naturalized and even gendered in the history of the colonization of India. Bhabha in "DissemiNation" discusses that nation is a narrative that encloses culture into its proper place, a nation, and argues that nation becomes a cultural force, while in actuality culture disseminates through nations and is hybridized. In the often-cited book *Imagined Communities*, Anderson already argues that a nation is an imagined community, socially constructed in order to establish a sense of belonging among people who share the values, cultures, and languages. This notion of nation makes the transnational space of mobility more plausible because destabilized borders make it easy for people to metaphorically wriggle through the borders. In other words, this notion makes essentialized national identities constructed by the idea of nation as a separate entity crumbled down. Further, this concept of nations as a narrative or an imagined community could destabilize and even dismantle linguistic and cultural borders, which can bring about translingual practices.

Nation, Language, and Monolingualism

One reason that a nation is a fluid state is that language and cultures that undergird a nation as a state are not so rigid as they are made to look. Before looking into the fluidity of language, it is important to understand that an entangled relation between language and nation has helped to sustain the notion of nation as reified separable entity. In *Translingual Practice: Global Englishes and Cosmopolitan Relations*, Canagarajah examines what cultural, economic, and academic climates have formulated and sustained the monolingual operation. According to Canagarajah, one of the cultural movements in the 17th century romanticized a given community by making strong links between the community and language spoken in the community. Language became the major adhesive that connected people within the community, and this shared language evidently helped them understand each other and share the same values. Since language and community were rooted in a certain geographical place in the romanticism age, these three factors, known as "Herderian triad," became inseparable. This triad makes it possible to maintain linguistic homogeneity, since a shared language in a community can be homogenized easily.

This mutual relation between a nation and a language in which both are contingent on each other has been questioned and debunked from different fields. Mühlhêusler points out from a post-colonial perspective that language "is a recent culture-specific notion associated with the rise of European nation-states and the Enlightenment. The notion of 'a language' makes little sense in most traditional societies" (qtd. in Makoni and Pennycook 440). This strong association between a language and a nation was fabricated, according to Bianco, because "nation states have absorbed and legitimized discourses and self-understanding as homogeneous and unilingual states" (330). Thus, a myth of one language in one nation constructs and holds the ideology that a nation's border can never be porous and in the same token a language in one nation has to be discrete from others in other communities or nations and so autonomous, even if people in a nation speak one language differently. In order to keep language discrete, it has to have some internal features, which can differentiate itself from other languages. Thus, "language" was invented as a pre-codified system and discrete and detachable from human beings, time, and context. The idea of transnational space undergirded by these concepts of nations and languages means that people just move between or over separable nations, which reinforces existing borders (Foucault), including borders among languages and cultures. It seems impossible that this transnational space can promote translingual practices, which presume that language is malleable and fluid.

However, Makoni and Pennycook in "Disinventing multilingualism" question the historical, cultural, and political underpinnings for this idea of language. Once linguistics is situated as part of the history of rhetorical traditions and philosophy, language cannot be a "putative science" (Makoni and Pennycook 439). Further, Pennycook argues for the disinvention of this constructed idea of language as a "putative system" and as one form of identity of a nation. Makoni and Pennycook propose lingua franca multilingualism (LFM), instead of multilingualism as plural monolingualism, to reconceptualize the notion of language. Lingua franca multilingualism is grounded in the notion that "languages are so deeply intertwined and fused into each other that the level of fluidity renders it difficult to determine any boundaries" (447).

Canagarajah's theorization of Lingua Franca English (LFE) as opposed to English as a Lingua Franca in "Lingua Franca English, Multilingual Communities, and Language Acquisition" also refutes this concept of language as a pre-codified system. In his discussion of LFE, insightfully Canagarajah states "LFE does not exist as a system 'out there,'" ("The Ecology" 91), which echoes Pennycook's criticism of "putative science," because "[i]t is constantly brought into being in each context of communication" ("Lingua Franca" 926). In other words, there is no set of rules of LFE that speakers need to acquire and follow, while English as a Lingua Franca is supposed to hold some "core features" (Canagarajah, *Translingual Practice* 63) that English language learners do not possess.

Both LFE and LFM are conceptually founded on fluidity of language in its broadest sense. Makoni and Pennycook's thought about fluidity is manifested in his idea of a "new sense of monolingualism" (444). This "new sense of monolingualism" is not the monolingualism that we know as the one that separates itself from other languages and is tied to nationalism. Of course, English and Arabic as languages, for instance, are different from each other in terms of corporeal aspects of the languages, such as their alphabets, and syntax. However, some of those differences, such as lexicon and semantics, are fluid and can be meshed and therefore a language is "a multilayered chain that is constantly combined and recombined" (Makoni and Pennycook 447). Theoretically speaking, this inseparability of language(s) might make only one language: that is Pennycook's "new sense of monolingualism."

Canagarajah emphasizes that LFE is a hybrid language in multilingual communities in "Lingua Franca English" and that in the book *Translingual Practice*, LFE is not even a language in its widely shared sense but a process. This hybrid language or a language as a process, at least, does not put a version of language as the pre-codified system on a throne and so could disrupt linguistic homogeneity. Further, Canagarajah develops the idea of multilingualism as plural monolingualism into translingualism. He explains that multilingualism "conceives of the relationship between languages in an additive manner," and so is not indicative of dynamic interactions between languages (*Translingual Practice* 8). Therefore, Canagarajah employs the term translingual, which in his conception can promote a more dynamic relation between languages and between languages and human beings.

The "new sense of monolingualism" and the hybrid language can unleash the simple but strong bond between a language and a nation and disrupts the myth that there is one language in one nation. When language becomes this fluid – or I should say that language is unleashed from its ideological burden – and nation as a concept does not hold as bordered, unified, and so fixed, translingual practices are never stabilized. Neither is transnational space. Next question to ask, then, is if transnational space is a precondition for translingual practices or a result of the practices.

Translingual Practice[2] and Space

Evidently several terms are used to describe a more dynamic relation between languages. Although translingual(ism) has been the main currency in various fields that study language, this section focuses on Canagarajah's translingual practice, Horner, et. al.'s translingual approach, and Pennycook's translingual English. Examining these scholar's different undertakings of "translingual" enables me to not only see how each one can dismantle linguistic homogeneity but also delve into the quality and nature of social spaces in which multilingual students can perform translingual practices to the end that they develop literacy in the process of transiting through different linguistic and semiotic repertoires at their disposal and negotiating meanings.

---

[2] It should be noted that there is the notion of translanguaging proposed from within the Bilingual Education discipline. According to Lee, Garcia's "*languaging* represents an emergent process of social interaction that does not merely draw from "language" but constitutes the "language" through ways in which it is practiced by individuals" (181). "languaging" changes its ontological stability, drawing more attention to human beings' agency over languages than translingual approach, translingual practice, and the poststructural mantra that we are constituted by language.

From composition studies, Horner, NeCamp and Donahue intensely criticize monolingualism in composition scholarship, such as publications in composition journals or presentations at conferences, which impose linguistic restrictions for acceptances (273). Horner, Lu, Royster and Trimbur in "Language Differences: Translingual Approach" propose that the composition studies field should take "the variety, fluidity, intermingling, and changeability of languages" (305) as a new norm. However, Horner, Lu, Royster and Trimbur at the same time contend that writers can and must negotiate the standardized rules depending on the contexts or rhetorical situations of writing (305). This translingual approach presumes that rhetorical situations determine which English to use, which will reinforce the division of different Englishes. As Lee astutely points out, Horner, et.al. take a pragmatist position and suggest that standard American English needs to be taught in composition classes (178). The term "translingual approach" is indicative that they employ the idea of translingual as allowing students to use different linguistic repertoire as an approach but in the end teach the standardized American English. Linguistic homogeneity is still kept unblemished, even if it is situated within certain rhetorical situations. The notion of language as a pre-codified set of rules is contained.

Pennycook, in "Translingual English," is most articulate about what this term "translingual" signifies or does not signify. He envisions the term "translingual English" as "include[ing] all uses of English. ... to acknowledge the interconnectedness of all English use" (8). Translingual for Pennycook signifies encompassment of all different Englishes, without pluralizing them simultaneously, instead creating a "new sense of monolingualism." "Syncretic cultural and linguistic practices" (Duff 60) makes translingual practices for Pennycook. Yet, this conception does not involve human beings, and because of that appears less dynamic, compared to Canagarajah's translingual practice. While Pennycook's arguments center on the concept of language, Canagarajah draws our attention to these language users' agencies over multiple languages.

Canagarajah's "translingual practice" promotes the students' agency in their communicative processes with languages and linguistic and semiotic resources at their disposal. Translingual practice does not refer to specific ways of using language, but rather to an orientation to language, which is to adopt multilingual repertoire and shuttle between different languages or different versions of one language. In this orientation[3], according to Canagarajah, people make meanings through negotiation in the contact zone; they do not adopt pre-

---

[3] This orientation also makes students use other semiotic affordances than language.

codified function of languages that exists without any human interaction ("Negotiating"). Canagarajah's idea of LFE is not a language per se, but rather "a social process that is constantly being remade from the semiotic resources available to speakers" (Pennycook, "Translingual English" 4). Pennycook's statement is apt here: "we do not speak languages, but rather deploy language resources at particular times and places" ("What might" 8). Thus, translingual practices demand multilinguals' agencies to implement.

Translingual(ism) operating on the idea of fluid language can theoretically dismantle monolingualism and disrupt linguistic homogeneity, especially when multilinguals can possess agencies over their linguistic repertoire. However, translingual practices are not always performed in some social, cultural, linguistic spaces. Some social spaces, but not all, make translingual practice happen, or make multilinguals have their ownership of language production, but others don't.

Contact Zone

Canagarajah designates social spaces where translingual practice can be performed as contact zones. He utilizes Mary Louisa Pratt's idea of contact zone in a different way from her. Pratt defines contact zones as "social spaces where cultures meet, clash, and grapple with each other, often in contexts of highly asymmetrical relations of power, such as colonialism, slavery, or their aftermaths" (34). This idea of contact zone highlights the power imbalance in contact zones. However, Canagarajah washes off this power imbalance Pratt points out in contact zones but instead takes them as generative spaces because the multilinguals bring in their linguistic and cultural assets in the zones to produce Lingua Franca English. Canagarajah presumes that contact zones are a precondition for translingual performance.

Canagarajah's contact zones are not the same as multilingual communities. Explaining the notion of the "Herderian triad" (*Translingual* 20), Canagarajah eloquently criticizes that community is almost always linked to a certain language and a place. Given the purpose of translingual practice, which is to perform and develop literacy in the process of shuttling among different linguistic repertoires at their disposal and negotiating meanings, the sense of community where values and language are shared among people would not nurture the translingual practice that is supposed to break the borders among languages. Canagarajah qualifies the space for translingual practice as "the contact zone without community" ("ESL Composition" 65).

The class that I taught held this quality of Canagarajah's contact zone and was able to perform translingual practices.

Course in Early College Program

I taught a writing course in the Early College Program provided by the community college in partnership with a couple of high schools in its community. The Early College Program allows eligible high school students to potentially earn up to 60 college credits for free. The course I taught there for two years is an accelerated Learning Community cluster course of ENG095 Writing Skills II, the last non-credit course in its developmental program, and ENG111 College Writing I, the credit-bearing introductory first year-writing course. This accelerated cluster provides students with more support and more detailed instructions for reading and writing than a regular stand-alone ENG111 for them to achieve learning outcomes for ENG111. This cluster is special among the same clusters offered to Early College program, in that the eligibility for this cluster is to finish ELL courses at the high school. The students enrolled in this cluster can be categorized as "former" ELL students, who predominantly immigrated from countries in South America.

I center this cluster on a theme of "Borderland," with three units: narrative essay, expository essay, and research project. We started to read the preface of Anzaldúa's *Borderland/LaFrontera* to get students to grasp the idea of a borderland, including psychological and linguistic borderlands, and to initiate into Anzaldúa's way to write in multiple languages. In the first unit, they tell a story about any kind of borderland they experienced. They struggled with expressing ideas and thoughts that they constructed from experiences they had in languages other than English. This is the unwritten purpose of this unit to have them think about what languages mean to them. This struggle made them take a risk of deploying their linguistic and semiotic resources.

In unit 2, I employed and tweaked the genre "Literacy Autobiography," which Canagarajah created ("ESL Composition"). I used this genre since it allows the students to inquire into their uses of different languages or different Englishes and also to make them realize their cultural and linguistic wealth. I tweaked it by adding a data-collection to the assignment so that they can investigate what these uses might reflect in a broader social context. To that end, students kept two-day logs about how they used languages differently depending on locations, contexts, etc. I gave an example of the list about different versions of languages that Anzaldúa uses from *Borderland/LaFrontera*. Examining the two-day logs as data, students analyze the numerous ways to use linguistic resources in an essay format. Latching onto the Unit 2 essay, in Unit 3, students delve into this idea of making choices in terms of linguistic repertoire by situating themselves in a larger society. They conduct interviews with their research participants and read sources to make their essays more rigorous and have them think more about what those choices reflect a larger society.

These assignments and activities that were conducted through translingual practices meet four General Education Outcomes for Academic Discourse: 1) Connect experiences, insights, and education in Unit 1, 2) Construct meaning through active listening, reading, speaking and writing in Unit 3, 3) Create work of personal and/or public value in Unit 2 and 3, and 4) Develop intercultural knowledge and competence in all three units (General Education). Translingual practices particularly brought students to accomplish outcome #2 and #4. The students constructed meanings through telling their stories and listening to others' experiences, which were performed in not just their "native" language but also rhetorical forms that they had gained through education back in their countries or from their cultures at large. These assignments also meet learning outcomes put forward by Learning Community at the community college. The first two units enable the students to "Connects relevant experience and academic knowledge." Reading Anzaldúa's snippets and reading the articles about code-meshing and code-switching allow them to "see (make) connections across disciplines, perspectives" (Learning Communities).

While these asset-based and translingual pedagogies enabled them to explore an issue and make meanings from exploration, by shuffling and mixing their linguistic and semiotic resources and negotiating meaning, translingual practices do not necessarily help them to achieve some learning outcomes in ENG111, such as "Revise writing for effective structure, support, and coherence," which is a U.S.- Euro centered way of knowledge production. It is a hasty conclusion to say that translingual practices are not "effective" enough for the multilinguals to gain the knowledge about the culturally constructed formula to produce knowledge. There will be more scaffolding for the effective structure and coherence in this curriculum needed.

Social space in my courses

The moment I step into a classroom on the first day of class, the gaze follows me as I head to the smartboard, put my bags and stacks of paper, turn on the computer, and set up everything I need to start a class, until I say "Hi, I'm your teacher. I teach writing." While pulling these two sentences out of my vocal cords, I catch the familiar facial expression of a couple of students, looking askance at me, probably because of my articulation, and knitting their eyebrows. I need to stop these gazes of doubt from weighing on my shoulders.

Writing courses that I teach usually make contact zones in Canagarajah's sense, where "cultures meet, clash, and grapple with each other" (Pratt). I still deal with the gaze of students in first-year writing courses. By dealing with these gazes, I create spaces where I encourage students to employ all possible versions of Englishes and their linguistic repertoire and to have students experience and understand what is more important than learning the standardized English. In first-year writing courses I teach at the college, cultural, linguistic, racial differences between me and other English teachers that students have had before would create a different classroom space, or a contact zone. My presence as an Asian who does not embody the U.S. educational culture as much as other U.S. born teachers do might have set a certain classroom climate. My presence, as a person who does not sound like other teachers at the high school, most likely influences this classroom atmosphere. I don't know how these differences affect the students' perception of me, their teacher of English. Yet, it is highly likely that this contact zone was different from those they experienced before, and so was unsettling for some of them as demonstrated by some students' behavior.

However, this contact zone, which is simply made of different cultural, linguistic, and racial attributes that each participant brings in, cannot simultaneously be the transnational space that I examined in the beginning of this chapter, where practices become fluid and so could be evolving. My mere presence does not make linguistic and cultural borders become porous and fluid features of the transnational space. The transnational space of fluidity and mobility is something that has to be proactively worked on because this space requires the endeavor to dismantle the established notions of nation and language, which is deeply embedded in and outside the classroom.

That being said, this contact zone, conceptually speaking, could be changed into a transnational space, since in the zone diverse languages can meet, merge, and infuse one another. Sheringham discusses that another feature of the transnational spaces is to free people from attachment to a place. This detachment might help to the job, to dismantle the notions of nation and language. Practices in this transnational space are supposed to be "carried out 'across spaces', excluding the possibility of attachments to specific 'places'" (Sheringham 61). This nature of transnational spaces promotes people and language more to continue to blur its border and disseminate themselves through the porous border, always in the state of "transition," or in the shifting in-between zones. This sounds liberating and promising socially, conceptually, and pedagogically.

Yet, Crang, Jackson, and Dwyer warn us that "we must not let the often-elite ideology of transnationalism blind us to the practical and emotional importance of attachments to and in place" (qtd. in Sheringham 63); otherwise, the blindness in real classrooms might hinder students from producing outcomes that these pedagogies intend to help them to accomplish. The questions emerging from this warning are whether multilingual speakers can perform translingual practices by detaching themselves from places without any sense of belonging, either literally or metaphorically, and if not, how and why it is important to be attached to places. These questionings enable me to qualify transnational spaces for translingual practices further. The multilinguals in the writing course for Early College Program performed translanguaging inside and outside the classroom setting. However, their languaging outside my class reveals the extent to which some sense of belonging or attachment to places matters for them to perform translingual practices.

Contact zones outside my class

Some critics of Canagarajah's theory argue that translingual practice can only take place in classroom settings (*Translingual Practice*). However, the multilingual students' two-day logs unexpectedly give me how they perform their translanguaging outside of the cluster course in their day-to-day shifting ground. Their logs show their linguistic dexterity that varies from one social space to another inside and outside of the school settings. For instance, in the logs one student entered, she found that she had seven ways to deploy linguistic and cultural resources: Work language, Spanmom language, Friendly language, Professional English, ReEnglish language, Familychapi language, and Catrachapi Language. She uses Spanish, Qui'che, some different expressions in Honduras, Guatemala, and Mexico, and English. "ReEnglsih" is a language for when she talked with her brother, who used to live in the U.S. but is now in his country. She said that "[W]e were joking in Spanish but he was in New York so he knows English and he wants to remember the English talking with me so I tried to talk with him in English." At her job, she speaks "Work language" that allows her to make recourses to some Spanish with her boss, who speaks Russian but understands some Spanish. According to the log, they both laugh at the Englishes they speak. The other logs also show how these multilinguals speak Spanish differently depending on location and context. The multilinguals in the class shuffle their linguistic resources and become more agentive in terms of which resources they use in numerous social, cultural, and linguistic spaces, or contact zones, which consist of many factors, such as location, time, context, intersubjectivity, and some unknowns. I think the multilinguals produced the transnational space of mobility in local contact zones.

Multilinguals in general, or for the exile, the immigrant, the refugee, and the asylum seeker in particular live in many different social spaces (Duff 61) without home in its traditional sense. People who leave their original place of residence seem to have to constantly situate themselves in "the in-between zones that are the shifting grounds on which the (doubly) exiled walk" (Minh-ha 70). These multilingual students seem to be adept at moving in and around "the in-between zones that are the shifting grounds" as Canagarajah's informants dynamically move across locations and contexts, using linguistic resources at their disposal. The multilingual students do not hold a strong attachment to a specific place, such as their home countries, as Sheringham argues.

However, there is a space that is not so porous and fluid in terms of their deployments of linguistic resources. For example, in one local social space where so-called native English speakers who also speak Spanish are a majority, some of the students did not do translanguaging as much as they did in other social spaces. The student, who has seven ways to deploy linguistic repertoires, described the context that she used "Professional English" in the school setting: "the teacher only speak English and the classroom also speak English, but they can also speak Spanish but I see how some of them believe that English is better than Spanish and they feel better than others who speak Spanish even they came from fathers who are Immigrants and talk Spanish." In that class, she did not deploy her rich linguistic and cultural resources. Some multilinguals do not cross over linguistic and cultural borders in some contact zones within local spaces, as did Canagarajah's informants. In those contact zones, some of the students do not even think of using their linguistic repertoires. It seems that the student loses the mobility that she owned in other "in-between zones that are the shifting grounds," such as her workplace.

Some multilingual students constantly situate themselves in "the in-between zones that are the shifting grounds" among different social spaces. This in-between zone can become a "bridge we call home" in Anzaldúa's theory of crossing in her book *This Bridge We Call Home* (Anzaldúa and Keating). However, since they do not belong to any social spaces in the same way they do in their original place of residence, this "home" as a bridge should not be the home in its traditional sense as a safe place. As Minnie Bruce Pratt points out that home in its narrowest sense can be dangerous because the concept could confine people in the space and exclude the "other" who may not share the same values and language in the space. Thus, the in-between shifting zones the multilinguals reside in as home is neither an actual geographical location nor a community that shares culture, language, history, etc. The in-between shifting zone as a "bridge we call home" that they are attached to could be a language that the multilinguals inhabit.

Language as home

Derrida contends that he inhabits a language and the language inhabits him (1). The language that he and multilinguals inhabit should not be simply regarded as native language. Their so-called native language is evolved and mixed, since some multilingual students do translanguaging every day to different degrees. Also, as Duff argues, proficiency of a language "cannot be equated to a single essentialized source location (or "home")" (64). The language they inhabit should not be tied to a home country as a geographical location. Nonetheless, they inhabit a language, which is constantly hybridized, as a "home."

Derrida investigates his relationship to the French language and theorizes the relationship between language and self and monolingualism at a metaphysical level. In the beginning of *Monolingualism of the Other*, his "literacy autobiography," Derrida makes the two seemingly contradicting propositions on language and people: 1) We only ever speak one language 2) we never speak only one language (7). These two propositions elucidate complicated relationships between people, or self, and languages.

Let me start with the second proposition. "We never speak only one language" in the sense that locations, contexts, time, and relation with others we communicate with would determine the tone, the lexicon, the syntax, and so forth that we deploy. Derrida adds to this proposition another feature that "there is no pure idiom"[4] (8). In each local context, we construct an idiom mixed with other idioms; hence, there is "no pure idiom" that is characteristic of an individual, of a language, and of relations between an individual and languages.

In a similar way, Derrida describes the first proposition ("we only ever speak one language") as having "rather one idiom only." When discussing people speaking several languages, Derrida asks "[b]ut do they not always do it with a view to an absolute idiom?" (67). Whatever languages they speak, they operate themselves in the languages, grounding themselves in the absolute idiom. This absolute idiom of relations between self - rather than social-cultural beings - and language enables us to make this proposition, "we only ever speak one language." This proposition brings us back to the second proposition. We could construe this second proposition in the way that since each of us has their own absolute idiom, a unique relationship to language, their language is not the same as mine; therefore, we never speak only one language.

These two seemingly contradicting relations between self and language also are consistent with the concept of language as not autonomous but discursive (we never speak only one language) and uncountable (we ever only speak one language). In other words, we are both multilingual – even if you speak "one" language – and simultaneously monolingual – even if you speak "some" languages.

---

[4] Here we do not need to argue about differences between language and idiom because Derrida explains that there are no internal features that distinguish language, idiom, and dialect.

However, this notion of monolingualism is neither the traditional sense of monolingualism nor Pennycook's "new sense of monolingualism." Neither notions fully take people, or self, into their accounts, although Pennycook discusses people's deployment of languages as a tool. Derrida's second proposition, however, centers on the relation between self and language. Derrida poetically describes the "pure idiom," the monolingual relationality between self and language in the second proposition. Derrida writes:

> But I am wrong, wrong to speak of a crossing and a place. For it is on the shores of the French language, uniquely, and neither inside nor outside it, on the unplaceable line of its coast that, since forever, and lastingly [a demeure], I wonder if one can love, enjoy oneself [jouir], pray, die from pain, or just die, plain and simple, in another language or without telling anyone about it, without even speaking at all (2).

In this depiction, Derrida's self does not belong to language in the sense that he can feel at home with the language, since its border is constantly shifting. Although Chow interprets that Derrida names his monolingualism as "absolute habitat" (217), Derrida does not take his monolingualism as a home in its traditional sense. In the very beginning, Derrida states "I am monolingual. My monolingualism dwells, and I call it my dwelling" (1), but the autobiographical work rolls out, he digs into this idea of "dwelling." Language constantly evolves and changes since it ebbs and flows, in Derrida's conceptualization of language. If language is a system and sits still somewhere autonomously, the self could reach it and stay there. However, that's not the way the relation operates in Derrida's view. Derrida describes this fluid relationality as "inalienable alienation" (25), since we neither totally belong in a language nor are we completely outside of it. He explains this idea of the inalienable alienation this way: "I have only one language and it is not mine" (25). Derrida's monolingualism lies in a unique inalienable alienation with language(s).

Some of the multilingual students' literacy autobiographies and their two-days logs show that they dwell in this relationship with their languages. The relationship with language could free them from the dwelling because it is alienable and bring them to shuttle numerous linguistics and semiotic resources, such as expressions, lexicons, syntax and so on. At the same time, the inalienable relationship sometimes could prevent them from deploying some linguistic resources that are "foreign" to their languages. The student who has the seven ways to deploy linguistic repertoires sometimes dwell in a language, other times alienate herself from that, and some other times deploy available linguistic resources more freely. As the quote from Derrida illustrates so well, the border of a language is changing like water on the shore and so make him find himself both in and outside of the language. This attachment to language as home is inevitable, wherever language is deployed.

Agency

This contradicting nature of this relationship explains one of the differences between Derrida and Canagarajah in terms of fluidity of language and agency. Derrida's theory of language in general needs to be understood and employed along with his conceptualization of self. Defined in a very reductionist way, self in Derrida's thinking is an effect of the discourses available to people. In other words, people are constituted by language. In the description of the fluidity of language by Derrida, human beings are not actively involved in the construction of the fluidity of language. The fluidity lies in the relation between self and language. On the other hand, Canagarajah's translingual practice postulates the innate agency of human beings, regardless of social spaces in which they are found. For Canagarajah, multilinguals are able to constitute language by adding, imposing, mixing, coining linguistic repertoire.

However, as the multilingual students in my course proved, the agency of language users is not always active. One student used English with a counselor, instead of Spanish, even if the counselor spoke Spanish. She said that "I feel more comfortable with her speaking English because there are some topics that I only know how to explain in English." She deliberately chose which linguistic sources to use, depending on subjects. Another multilingual student described and explained the complexity of speaking Spanish, English, and Korean. Her use of linguistic resources mostly hinged on the relationships with persons she talked to and on contexts. In a contact zone with the monolingual, this student seemed to have some degree of agency in choosing some words that she thought would impress the monolingual: "When I talk with my Chemistry teacher, I use some fancy words, and some scientific words because I want to be respect with him, and I try to expand my vocabulary." Although that choice reflects the hierarchy of syntax, vocabulary, etc. in English, she did not lose agency because her culture directed her to make the decision. On the other hand, the student, who has the seven ways of deploying linguistic and cultural repertoires, seemed to lose some channel to the resources in the contact zone where some classmates dominantly spoke English even if they spoke Spanish, too. This student interpreted these classmates' language use: "What makes me think is that they are racist and they are not proud of speak Spanish or maybe they feel ashamed of speak Spanish."

Thus, some contact zones are not necessarily generative as Canagarajah hopes because the zones are saturated with power imbalances, which deprive the multilinguals of chances to perform a form of translingual practice. Some of the students feel less for not being as "proficient" as so-called native English speakers. This feeling can be evoked in contact zones where some native English speakers exert more power over non-native English speakers by projecting that English holds culturally higher asset. Or other multilinguals hierarchize their multiple languages in some contact zones as this student's classmates did, which also affect the agency of some other multilinguals. As Mary L. Pratt explicates, some contact zones are "of highly asymmetrical relations of power, such as colonialism, slavery, or their aftermaths" (34). The contact zone in which the student was placed was infused with power and status. The power imbalance would move the multilinguals in my class to hanker back for the language as home. The student dwells in the place, a language from which she cannot alienate herself, but simultaneously needs to in-alienate herself because of the nature of the contact zone. This in-alienation leads to a lack of agency. Contact zones that hold imbalances of power cannot be the transnational space because the imbalance took away the agencies.

If the contact zone in my class was changed into transnational space, that would be because the power that most English teachers exert as knowledge holders or gatekeepers, with or without knowing, did not circulate itself in the zones. Throughout a given semester, I was not constantly conscious of creating a transnational space. However, I spent the whole semester presenting myself as a teacher of writing and a learner of languages as well. This presentation of my linguistic identity seemed to help me to relinquish the unnecessary power. I do work on "highly asymmetrical relations of power" between teachers and students in classrooms. Therefore, what I make sure through the semester is that I am privileged to be a part of their writing and thinking process.

I do not argue that this is the way to create the transnational space of mobility and fluidity. But I do argue that transnational space is a product of labor, such as translingual practices, but not a precondition for the practices. Transnational space for translingual practices should be a space where the relationality with language, inalienable alienation, is not impaired by the power imbalance. Therefore, in order to produce transnational space, in general, people involved there should at least grapple with dismantling the power imbalance that impacts or disfranchises a certain group of people in the space.

Words in Closing

This changing intricate relationship between language and self and the fluctuating performance of the multilinguals' translanguaging that reflect the relationship will make instructors of first year writing courses more alert to their linguistic identities and their relationship with English in the classrooms. Classrooms are also social spaces and could not be free from the power relationship between addressers and addressed. However, the power relationship is not set in the stone. The nature of the spaces is in constant influx depending on who addresses whom with what kind of power to be exerted (Ellsworth). Social spaces, whether they are considered contact zones or transnational spaces, are multifaceted or multidimensional. They don't offer any predetermined nature for human beings there. The nature of social spaces can be created and transformed by changing intersubjectivity among people involved and a power relation that is entailed from the intersubjectivity. Instructors of writing courses must be aware that they are in "volatile social space-between" (Ellsworth 38).

Not only will instructors' identities, especially linguistic ones, affect the nature of classrooms, but also the multilingual learners' perception of the relationship between their instructors and English will affect it. They will examine and assess if their instructors are gatekeepers of the language, multilinguals, monolinguals, or native speakers. One of Canagarajah's academic endeavors is to dismantle the binary between native speakers and non-native speakers. I would think that his theorization of translingual accomplishes that. However, differences between native speakers and non-native speakers do exist for some people, including multilingual students. They take for granted these notions of language as autonomously pre-codified sets and native speakers as owners of the language. Multilingual students' – any student is, I would argue, multilingual – assessments of the relationship between their instructors and English shape the social spaces and their relationship with language, inalienable alienation, in classrooms in various ways. Depending on how instructors address their students, their agency over language, either innate or given, might not be activated to perform translanguaging. All these factors of instructors' linguistic identities, students' perceptions of the instructors' relationship with the language, and the modes of address make the spaces volatile. Ellsworth argues that "*all* modes of address misfire one way or another. I never "am" the "who" that a pedagogical address thinks I am. But then again, I never am the who that *I* think I am either" (8). Likewise, the students never are the who that a pedagogical address thinks they are, nor the who that they think they are. To ease this volatility, it is crucial to be aware that instructors of writing, who are persuaded by this translingual pedagogy or translanguaging performance, do not teach English because language is not a separate system but a process; instead, instructors teach writing as thinking through languaging.

Works Cited

Anderson, Benedict. *Imagined Communities: Reflections on the Origin and Spread of Nationalism.* Revised ed., Verso, 2016.

Anzaldúa, Gloria E. *Borderlands/La frontera: The New Mestiza.* Aunt Lute Books, 1987.

Anzaludra, Gloria E., and AnaLouise Keating, editors. *This Bridge We Call Home: Radical Visions for Transformation.* Routledge, 2002.

Beverley, John. "The Margin at the Center: On *Testimonio* (Testimonial Narrative)." *De/Colonizing the Subject: The Politics of Gender in Women's Autobiography,* edited by Sidonie Smith and Julia Watson. University of Minnesota Press, 1992, pp. 91-114.

Bhabha, Homi. K. "DissemiNaion: Time, Narrative, and the Margins of the Modern Nation." *Nation and Narration.* Routledge, 1990, pp. 291-322.

Bianco, Joseph Lo. "A Celebration of Language Diversity, Language Policy, and Politics in Education." *Review of Research in Education,* vol. 38, 2014, pp. 312-33.

Canagarajah, Suresh. "ESL Composition as A Literate Art of The Contact Zone." *First-Year Composition: From Theory to Practice,* edited by Deborah Teague and Ron Lunsford, 2014, Parlor Press, pp. 27-48.

—. "Lingua Franca English, Multilingual Communities, and Language Acquisition." *The Modern Language Journal, Focus Issue: Second Language Acquisition Reconceptualized?* vol. 91, 2007, pp. 923-939.

—. "Negotiating Translingual Literacy: An Enactment." *Research in the Teaching of English,* vol. 48, no. 1, August 2013, pp. 40-67.

—. "The Ecology of Global English." *International Multilingual Research Journal,* vol.1, no. 2, 2007, pp.89-100.

—. *Translingual Practice: Global Englishes And Cosmopolitan Relations.* Routledge, 2013.

Chow, Rey. "Reading Derrida on Being Monolinugal." *New Literary History,* vol. 39, no. 2, Spring 2018, pp. 217-231.

Conference on Coll. Composition and Communication, Urbana, IL. "Students' Rights to Their Own Language." *College Composition and Communication,* vol. 25, 1974. EBSCOhost.

Dahinden, Janine. "The Dynamics of Migrants' Transnational Formations: Between Mobility and Locality." *Diaspora and Transnationalism: Concepts, Theories, and Methods"* edited by Rainer Baubock and Thomas Faist. Amsterdam University Press, 2010, pp. 51-72.

Derrida, Jacques. *Monolingualism of the Other or The Prosthesis of Origin.* Translated by Patrick Mensah. Stanford UP, 1998.

Duff, Patricia. A. "Transnationalism, Multilingualism, and Identity." *Annual Review of Applied Linguistics,* vol. 35, 2015, pp. 57-80.

Ellsworth, Elizabeth. *Teaching Positions: Difference, Pedagogy, and the Power of Address.* Teachers College Press, 1997.

Faist, Thomas. "Diaspora and Transnationalism: What Kind of Dance Partners?" *Diaspora and Transnationalism: Concepts, Theories, and Methods,"* edited by Rainer Baubock and Thomas Faist. Amsterdam University Press, 2010, pp. 9- 34. www.jstor.org/stable/j.ctt46mz31.4.

Foucault, Michel. "A Preface to Transgression." *Language, Counter-Memory, Practice: Selected Essays and Interviews*, edited by Donald F. Bouchard and translated by Donald F. Bouchard and Sherry Simon. Cornel UP, 1977, pp. 29-52.

General Education at Bunker Hill Community College. https://www.bhcc.edu /programsofstudy/generaleducationrequirements/ Accessed 11 Nov 2020.

Giroux, Henry A. *Border Crossings: Cultural Workers and the Politics of Education.* Routledge, 1993.

Grewal, Inderpal. "Becoming American: The Novel and the Diaspora." *Transnational America: Feminism, Diaporas, Neoliberalisms.* Duke University Press, 2005, pp. 35-79.

Hemphill, David., and Erin Blakely. "Globalization, Transnationality, and Citizen-Consumers." *Counterpoints*, vol. 456, 2015, pp. 79-104.

Horner, Bruce., et al. "Language Difference in Writing; Toward a Translingual Approach." *Faculty Scholarship*, 2011, The University of Louisville's Institutional Repository, pp. 303-321.

Horner, Bruce., et al. "Toward a Multilingual Composition Scholarship: From English Only to a Translingual Norm." *CCC*, vol. 63, no. 2, December 2011, pp. 269-300.

Kachru, Yamuna. "Monolingual Bias in SLA Research." *TESOL Quarterly*, vol. 28, no. 4, Winter 1994, pp. 795-800.

Learning Community Outcomes. Provided in the packet of "Professional Development on ESL Integrated Skills Courses" at Bunker Hill Community College, March 9, 2019.

Lee, Jerry W. "Beyond Translingual Writing." *College English*, vol. 79, no. 2, November 2016, pp. 174-195.

Lyiscott, Jamila. "3 Ways to Speak English." *TED: Ideas Word Spreading*, February 2014, www.ted.com/talks/jamila_lyiscott_3_ways_to_speak_engli sh?language=en

Makoni, Sinfree., and Alastair Pennycook. "Disinventing Multilingualism: From Monological Multilingualism to Multilingua Francas." *The Routledge Handbook of Multilingualism*, edited by Marilyn Martin-Jones, Adrian Blackledge and Angela Crees. Routledge, 2012, pp.439-453.

Martin, Biddy., and Chandra T. Mohanty. "Feminist Politics: What's Home Got to Do with It?" *Feminist Studies/Critical Studies: Language, Discourse, Society*, edited by de Lauretis T. Palgrave Macmillan, 1986, pp. 191-212.

May, Stephen., editor. *The Multilingual Turn.* Kindle ed. Routledge. 2014.

McWhorter, John. "What's a Language, Anyway?" *The Atlantic*, 19 Jan. 2016, www.theatlantic.com/international/archive/2016/01/difference-between-language-dialect/424704/

Minh-ha, Trinh. T. *Elsewhere, Within Here: Immigration, Refugeeism And The Boundary Event.* Routledge, 2011, New York and London.

Mohanty, Chandra. T. "Crafting Feminist Genealogy: On the Geography and politics of Home, Nation, and Community." *Talking Visions: Multicultural*

Feminism in a Transnational Age, edited by Ella Shohat, MIT Press, 2001, pp. 485-500.

Pathak, Zakia. "A Pedagogy for Postcolonial Feminists." *Feminists Theorize the Political*, edited by Judith Butler and Joan W. Scott. Routledge, 1992, pp. 426-444.

Pennycook, Alastair. "Translingual English." *Australian Review of Applied Linguistics*, vol. 31, no. 3, Monash University, 2008, pp. 30.1-30.9.

—. "What might translingual education look like?" *Babel*, vol. 47, no. 1, 2012, p. 4+. Gale Academic OneFile, link-gale-com.ezproxy.neu.edu/apps/doc/A 308598678/AONE?u=mlin_b_northest&sid=AONE&xid=54c90d22. Accessed 8 Mar. 2020.

Pratt, Mary. L. "Arts of The Contact Zone." *Profession*, 1991, pp. 33-40.

Pratt, Minnie. B. "Identity: Skin Blood Heart." *Rebellion: Essays 1980-1991*. Firebrand Books, 1991, pp. 27-77.

Sheringham, Oliver. "A Transnational Space? Transnational Practices, Place-Based Identity and the Making of 'Home' among Brazilians in Gort, Ireland." *Portuguese Studies*, vol. 26, no. 1. 2010, pp. 60 – 78.

Shiller, Nina. G. "A Global Perspective on Transnational Migration: Theorizing Migration without Methodological Nationalism." *Diaspora and Transnationalism: Concepts, Theories, and Methods*, edited by Rainer Baubock and Thomas Faist, Amsterdam University Press, 2010, pp. 109-130.

Young, Vershawn A. "Introduction: Are You a Part of the Conversation?" *Other People's English: Code-Meshing, Code-Switching, an African American Literacy*, edited by Vershawn Ashanti Young., et al. Teachers College Press, 2014, pp. 1-14.

Part 2.
Creating Transnational Space through Pedagogical Designs Focused on Genre

In this section, the authors offer us unique writing program and course design models that specifically apply transnational modes of learning. They designed their modules around the rhetorical ideas of genre. While other sections of this volume have focused on specific writing assignments or curriculum, these authors take us through course structures intended to highlight principles of genre as a means of creating transnational space. These spaces are created by deconstructing and then restructuring ideas of language, nationality, and culture.

This section also includes authors who share similarities in that their course designs reflect their own transnationality. The transnational spaces in which they work are in part constructed by their own bodies. For Writing Program Administrators, Andrew Hollinger and Colin Charlton, their whiteness in congruence with the perceptions of "Standard English" play a role in redefining a writing program that resides in a Hispanic Serving Institution along the Texas-Mexico border. Their focus is to work with students' perception of "language" and "writing" as specific genres or constructs that are not universal. Andrew and Colin use Ryan Skinnel's *genitive history* methodology to create a transnational writing program reflective of the transnational ecology where their writing program operates. Their work is particularly insightful for transnational pedagogy because it offers readers insight into designing a writing program from scratch (the university where they teach was founded in 2013). Their purpose is "to maintain the trans-movements or crossings in ongoing discussions across the -hoods of the self, of age, of physical and mental geographies ... of the tongues tamed, untamed, and those uttering in the in-between spaces we can witness more than name." The authors breakdown their writing program into the areas where heuristics were applied: creating a writing program identity, following a list of hiring practices, building (or the perpetual building of) curriculum, and offering professional development. These insights offer administrators means of creating transnational writing programs that subsequently infer transnational writing classrooms.

Asmita Ghimire and Elizabethada Wright construct a hypothesized curriculum that de-naturalizes everyone's "English" by reframing everyone's English as alien. *All Writers Have More Englishes to Learn* offers Ghimire's perspective as a transnational graduate assistant teaching writing students in the midwest where "awareness and acceptance of Englishes in the FYC classes require the comprehension of transnational practices." Like Colin and Hollinger's research, these authors focus on threshold concepts depicted in *Naming What We Know* by Linda Adler-Kassner and Elizabeth Wardle. Ghimire and Wright specifically address the threshold concepts concerning identities and genre. The authors propose assignments and pedagogies that are founded upon ideas from William Lalicker, Patricia Bizzell, Trimbur, Horner, NeCamp, and Donahue. The authors have synthesized the ideas of genre, identity, and have used their own transnational relationship to offer a compelling case to their students that challenges the students' preconceived notions of writing while providing space for non-native speakers of English a means of teaching rhetoric outside the constructs of North American rhetoric.

Demet Yigitbilek's chapter, *Translingual and Transnational Pedagogies Enacted: Linguistic and Cultural Trajectory Narratives in FYC*, presents a scenario similar to Ghimire's. Yigitbilek is a Turkish citizen teaching in a university in the midwest where the students' whiteness reinforces ideas of "Standard English." She uses the transnationality of her own body to create transnational spaces in the classroom to undermine and challenge the misconceptions of "Standard English" and reinforce concepts of genre. Yigitbilek teaches her students genre concerning cultural and linguistic diversity using writing assignments that increase their awareness of how culture and identity shapes one's literacy. She uses theoretical grounding from Anzaldúa and takes up Matsuda's charge to fill the gaps of theorization via practice in interdisciplinary contexts to design her course with the theme *Language and/as Identity*. Yigitbilek's approach is unique in that she represents a transnational linguistic history and teaches classrooms where students are ¾ homogeneous. Her goal, like Ghimire and Wright's, is to break stereotypes of "Standard English" by implementing assignments that require students to reflect on their own linguistic history. Where other chapters in this volume focus on encouraging transnational spaces in transnational environments, Yigitbilek's research is in developing translingual and transnational curriculum through genre in a seemingly *homogenous* ecology. Her unique position as a translingual instructor is used to show the students how their thinking of language and cultural homogeneity is genre based.

The research in this section offers valuable insight into course design strategies that use threshold constructs of genre to create transnational spaces. Readers interested in designing writing courses that are transnational in theme will benefit from this section.

Chapter 4

A Confluence of Xings: A Nested Heuristic for Developing and Networking Individual, Programmatic, and Institutional Spaces of Transnational Work

Andrew Hollinger and Colin Charlton

University of Texas Rio Grande Valley

Abstract: The authors situate the development of a transnational space programmatically. They discuss how the First-Year Writing Program (WP) at UTRGV developed (and continues to develop, affirm, renew) an identity as a translingual and transnational program, establishing an institutional ethos, support, authority for teachers and students as they work to create their own classroom environments. In particular, the WP has specifically addressed (and continues to address) antiracist pedagogy, social justice, and inclusive writing and languaging practices. The authors close the discussion with a heuristic for establishing a program as a transnational space to foster and support that environment at the classroom level.

Keywords: writing program, curriculum, transnational, translingual, heuristic, positionality, professional development, Hispanic Serving Institution (HSI)

***

"Until I am free to write bilingually and to switch codes without having always to translate, while I still have to speak English or Spanish when I would rather speak Spanglish, and as long as I have to accommodate the English speakers rather than having them accommodate me, my tongue will be illegitimate. I will no longer be made to feel ashamed of existing. I will have my voice: Indian, Spanish, white. I will have my

serpent's tongue—my woman's voice, my sexual voice, my poet's
voice. I will overcome the tradition of silence."

—Gloria Anzaldúa
The Borderlands/La Frontera: The New Mestiza

"Through writing, writers come to develop and perform identities in
relation to the interests, beliefs, and values of the communities they
engage with, understanding the possibilities for selfhood available in
those communities. The act of writing, then, is not so much about
using a particular set of skills as it is about becoming a particular kind
of person, about developing a sense of who we are."

—Kevin Roozen
"Writing is Linked to Identity," *Naming What We Know*

Every few years *The Chronicle of Higher Education* publishes a "think" piece
by some frustrated writing teacher suggesting that "students can't write a clear
sentence to save their lives" (Teller) and so "we must get back to basics in our
writing instruction" (Jenkins, "Basics") because "one of the best things we can
do for students is to help them master standard English" (Jenkins, "Standard
English"). Rob Jenkins takes it further by recognizing there have been
arguments "more recently that the English language is discriminatory, even
racist. I understand the reasoning and sympathize to a degree—but ultimately
reject those arguments" ("Standard English"). Aside from completely
misrepresenting the research about language and the arguments surrounding
Standard Academic English, Jenkins thoroughly embodies Asao Inoue's claim
in his 2019 4Cs keynote about "the problem of the conditions of White
language supremacy, not just in our society and schools, but in our own
minds, in our habits of mind, in our dispositions, our bodies, our *habitus*, in
the discursive, bodily, and performative ways we use and judge language. This
means, many of us can acknowledge White language supremacy as the status
quo in our classrooms and society, but not see all of it, and so perpetuate it"
(6). If it is fundamental that writing is "understanding the possibilities for
selfhood available in [our] communities" (Roozen 50-51), then programs and
instructors who restrict elements of language are effectively limiting the
possibilities for selfhood available in our/the students' academic and
professional communities through which their identities are becoming.
Perhaps even more sad and "sinister" are the ways that discursive limits on
the "discursive, bodily, and performative ways we use and judge language"
(Inoue 6) impede the ingenious interaction of the unfamiliar or disconnected
discourses of our lives. They dampen the potential cross-pollination of

languages within one person, say, a Spanish-speaking father tutoring geometry to his kids at home who is also a biology lab report-writing student in an English-speaking lab session on campus. Limiting languaged selfhoods seems, at the very least, problematic, but more likely a continuation of hegemonic, corporate, and racial hierarchies.

We should want better for our students, especially in first-year writing (FYW). First-year writing should be an opportunity for students to take creative and academic risks, to test ideas, to find themselves belonging to a scholarly community rather than existing at its fringes. At UTRGV, first-year writing is not a gatekeeping course sequence so much as an experiment "about becoming a particular kind of person, about developing a sense of who [the students] are" (Roozen 51). And we encourage students to bring their full range of identities and experiences to bear on their writing and their scholarship. Although far from perfect, the FYW course sequence at UTRGV is designed to be *translingual* and *transnational*. The sequence is translingual in the sense that it approaches "language not as a barrier to overcome or as a problem to manage, but as a resource for producing meaning in writing, speaking, reading, and listening" (Horner, et al. 303). The sequence is transnational in the sense that it makes space for "compelling opportunities to develop a more comprehensive understanding of the heterogeneity and fluctuating nature of the writing experienced in writing classes" (Martins 12). Our FYW assignments, their sequencing, and their individual design are positioned as writing prompts that treat language as a resource and writing as an oscillating tool of inquiry, standardization, resistance, and discursive reflection.

When the courses are successful, it is because the writing program (the faculty, policies, curriculum, events, initiatives, and so on) has embraced a translingual and transnational position. This *abrazo* is not a simple encircling, nor is it established and consistent over time. We've seen, at least since our history of this program began in 2005, the oscillations in desired writing outcomes among some area of language/writing representing "standards," some area representing "inclusion" or "expansion" and a third plateau which we can think of as a desire for neutrality, passive resting, or repetition. While this perception of a program's representation of language values is reminiscent of Raymond Williams' analysis of culture and its internal differentiation among residual, dominant, and emergent cultural formations as a means by which we can understand the relationship between alternative value systems or cultural practices and dominant norms, we believe it goes further in suggesting that these cultural formations are complex and on-going almost outside chronology, in part because large writing programs like the one we administer and participate in include such a variety of expertise, cultural and academic entry points, and professional pedagogical goals.

Amidst such a program of perpetual motion at the individual level, we believe our overall success as a *program* lies in the articulation of these oscillations alongside our outcomes and our professional development discussions. We, as teacher-colleagues and program administrators, see it as our responsibility to maintain the trans- movements or crossings in ongoing discussions across the -hoods of the self, of age, of physical and mental geographies . . . of the tongues tamed, untamed, and those uttering in the in-between spaces we can witness more than a name.

What we offer here is a heuristic for developing a/our writing program, thoughtful and purposeful in its approach to language and "the possibilities for selfhood" we are introducing to our students, while still flexible enough to respond to the specific conditions at any institution. In this way, we borrow from Ryan Skinnell's *genitive history* methodology and present *genitive* examples of the work done at the University of Texas Rio Grande Valley (UTRGV). That is, we want to recognize that UTRGV is a unique rhetorical ecology and our experiences, initiatives, and activities may not be directly transplantable to other institutions. Our work is local, *genitive* in the sense that UTRGV's experiences belong to the writing program at UTRGV. Skinnell argues, however, that "the genitive case represents a systematic, 'non-accidental' grouping of integrally related components, which can be usefully considered in their particularities, as well as in relation to, and as a reflection of, the larger category" (42). Our hope is that the particularities of our UTRGV labors can, in some way, indicate "a categorical relationship—a group affiliation with identifiable characteristics that maintain across multiple instances" while "each individual relationship...may play out in radically differing ways...without invalidating the categorical association" (Skinnell 42). We understand there is a lot at stake for and in writing instruction. Asao Inoue says the "key" to developing more compassionate, balanced, racially aware classrooms "is changing the structures, cutting the steel bars, altering the ecology, in which your biases function in your classrooms and communities" (11-12). UTRGV, from its inception (and before), has been serious about "altering the ecology" so that students find themselves as full, enmeshed stakeholders in their education rather than passive participants in a hegemonic ideal.

Context at UTRGV

UTRGV is a Hispanic Serving Institute (HSI) that opened its doors in 2015, merging from the legacy institutions University of Texas-Pan American in Edinburg, Texas, and University of Texas at Brownsville in Brownsville, Texas. In 2015, 92% (3,855/4,181) of entering first-year students identified as Hispanic ("Fall 2015 UTRGV Freshman Profile"). In 2019, 93.8% (4,497/4,793) of entering first-year students identified as Hispanic, a growth both in overall enrollment and percentage of students identifying as Hispanic ("Fall 2019 UTRGV Freshman Profile").

An important dimension of the university's identity as an HSI is an understanding of the linguistic and cultural complexity of the student population that underlies the HSI categorization. While the strategic plan of the university articulated the identity of UTRGV as bilingual, bicultural, biliterate (B3) when it began, the practical and shared definition of those words is still underway by a university task force. Beside that work at the institutional level, the students that inhabit that emergent, liminal, and ideological space have different levels of oral proficiency (in English and Spanish), different levels of writing proficiency (in English and Spanish), and can inhabit very few or very many discourse communities that deploy multiple and often mixed languages. The ways in which and the reasons for using a specific language, discourse, or register in a certain context are complex rhetorical acts that we are witness to and agents in every time a new student enters a writing classroom. Those classrooms are sites of exposure (to a new school, to dominant school discourses, to unfamiliar readings and writings) and sites of potential choices (in writing and saying) that we, as translingually-attuned teachers have to make the part of the writing subject of the class.

The first-year writing program is a semi-independent writing program, existing in the Department of Writing & Language Studies (WLS) alongside the areas of rhetoric and composition, applied linguistics, Spanish, translation and interpreting, and language acquisition (Spanish and nine other languages). The faculty cohort is large: 33 full-time faculty on three-year renewable contracts with an advancement pathway, 11 tenured and tenure-track rhetoric and composition faculty that also occasionally teach first-year writing courses, and 4-6 adjunct lecturers on one-year contracts. Of the 33 full time writing program lecturers, 66.7% (22/33) identify as Latinx. We should also note, as an important disclosure practice connected to conscientious languaging and anti-racist practices, the WLS department chair and the coordinator of the first-year writing program (the authors of this chapter) are white. Inoue notes that white scholars and administrators "do not control their Whiteness. But they do control how they deploy it, how they make it visible and the privileges of leadership it conveys to them" (Inoue 16). Perhaps the foundational element of our heuristic is deliberateness and acknowledgement. If the insidious thing about language supremacy is that instructors and administrators continue to promote it unwittingly, as "*habitus*" (Inoue 8), then the first and most direct thing we can do as instructors and administrators is be aware and signify our awareness. In every aspect of our teaching and programmatic work, we acknowledge our whiteness and the privileges that accompany that. Our work comprises deliberate and considered compassion and conscientiousness.

Generative Xings, A Nested Heuristic

1. *Recognize and explore positionality and privilege*. Without acknowledging space, place, and privilege, any labor toward conscientiousness and compassion is incomplete.

We'll start with the Xings that probably weigh heaviest on our minds, and we'll unpack the lengthy administrative story of Colin's positionality as a way of explaining how we see and explore privilege publicly. A few years into his job as an Assistant Professor, he became an Assistant Coordinator of Developmental English (situated under the first-year writing program) and a member, and eventual chair, of the university's Program Review Committee. The Assistant Coordinator gig (received because of expertise) led to a large grant to reform our support of transitional and non-college-ready students as readers and writers, and the committee gig (received because of people's perception of his ability to get work done) led to a greater understanding of program design, maintenance, review, and revision in the contexts of Texas educational policy and the RGV's student (and cultural) pipeline. As a member of and a leader in the writing program curriculum, his position was pretty clear. He and many of the rhetoric and composition specialists supported a metacognitive, writing studies approach to developmental courses, and that was juxtaposed with a large number of lecturers and part-time teachers with literature and creative writing backgrounds and a consistent murmur from them and many in the university about the need for better academic English. This was 2007-2008. The Conference on College Composition and Communication had adopted the Students' Rights to Their Own Language statement thirty-three years prior and the statement on Second Language Writers and Writing statement in 2001. For the vast majority of colleagues teaching first-year writing, we were circulating statements and approaches that were new and threatening to the status quo even though those statements were well established by the respective experts in rhetoric and writing disciplines.

Let's jump forward--through Colin's short stint as the full writing program coordinator from 2013-2015 to being the chair of a new department of Writing & Language Studies in a new university in a new College of Liberal Arts. Some of the same grumblings about standards circulated, but our departmental and program partnerships across the university were working to address those recycled questions about essays, grammar, student writing, and what people should be learning. But this new chair role was in support of experts in rhetoric, linguistics, Spanish, Asian Studies, and more, which made his positionality even more integral to the health and growth of a complex system.

Relatively few rhetoric and writing faculty have the option to work in a stand-alone writing department or program, seemingly in charge of its own destiny when it comes to the business of teaching writing. The Association of Rhetoric & Writing Studies (rhetoricandwriting.org) maintains a growing list of diverse programs and departments that self-identify as stand-alone. Even fewer programs, however, will have Colin's experience with writing and language specialists (rhetoric faculty alongside language acquisition faculty alongside linguistics faculty alongside first-year writing lecturers with rhetoric or literature or creative writing backgrounds) inhabiting the same institutional space. It puts positionality in sharp relief. Here's what we mean in terms of sharp relief: An FYW lecturer proposes revising an extra-curricular reading workshop series to possibly meet the needs of students beyond the current focus of reading in first-year writing classes. By the end of the day, what might be a writing program thought about second-language reading butts up against a question about course caps in language acquisition courses because of the Chinese instructional practice in pictograms. That slams into a gap in an L2's specialist's awareness of genre theory from the 1970s in rhetoric and composition that occurs while researching a job candidate. Thoughts then turn a corner and get somewhat surprised by a Spanish acquisition instructor for non-heritage learners still depending on fill-in-the-blank scantron tests.

Faced with so many disciplines and disciplinary backgrounds, trajectories, and pedigrees, the mantra worth adopting is a simple one: *nothing is ever enough, so keep talking about what and why with everyone.* You can never overwrite your privilege, and you are also not in control of how it is perceived, how we are perceived as writers and language-users in our programs and departments even as we explore the boundaries of student language, of multi- and trans-lingual minds, and interdisciplinary knowledge-making. As leaders, we are living an existence among experts who need to demonstrate their expertise and students who want an expertise while awash in discourses they may understand, for the most part, implicitly. The answer is not to be transparent. Transparency is fiction at best. What is needed is context and dialogue, and that means supporting and designing a place where understanding our rhetorical ecologies is everyday and commonplace for both our students and diverse faculty.

As a designer and artist, Colin embraces hybrids. To represent that which is right there in front of his eyes, no matter how filtered, is a slow and unsatisfying death of invention. He does not really like academic heroes, even in the related practice of epigraphs, but he understands how heroes and framing quotations serve a valuable function. And he was once fluent in French as an undergraduate double major in English and French (though perhaps that was more of a fluency in French film and history...). So even his language background smacks of privilege when dropped into the South Texas rhetorical ecology. When you mash that together with a complex university history, it leads to the need for a re-framing of language and identity by a chair responsible for fostering projects, aligning outcomes, appointing coordinators, overseeing policies and articulations of values, etc. So the resulting guiding questions he asks himself every week, almost in every student and faculty interaction, are these:

- What is the adaptive potential of what you're proposing/doing for yourself, for the students, for the faculty, for the department, for the university, or for the community? (a question of context-rich sustainability)

- How does it align with the outcomes for the programs we are all partners to? (a question of context-rich cohesion)

These questions are not intended to be platforms for the perpetuation of privilege. We're asking about adapting something, so we're promoting change, and we're talking about alignment, so we never escape the existing structure. We think the difference, to get rhetorical for a second, between these guiding principles and perpetuations of privilege is in the delivery and the memory of these questions. We're not proposing or asking these questions to perfect. We're asking them to find potential overlaps in thinking, identify uninvited perspectives, and seek a refined trans- space that can be read in many contexts.

To construct a transnational and translingual space in a writing classroom, then, you need to—and here the language is incredibly important—allow linked spaces to emerge throughout the system. We believe we can allow, and not direct or impose, trans-thinking by being the folks who ask, *how are we helping people adapt what they know to what they're learning to have a desired impact on a piece of the world they've identified a connection to? How does that world-building (though it may sound over-the-top) tie back to the relevant outcomes?* This is not an alignment for alignment's sake. It is alignment as a reflective act.

For the upcoming year, our department is undergoing a discussion of vision. We have a placeholder mission that represents the department's various educational stakeholders. But the vision for us is actually harder to develop because the vision that drove each area for five years was *survival.* We were in a primarily reactive state, and that goes for the first-year writing program even though it was developing with the growing university regardless of our assessment and program revisions. Its identity was undergoing a transition, and we weren't really sure how each change of common textbook or assignment sequence might impact the overall program identity. Currently, we are in a period of relative stability in which the exploration of a new showcase or event for the program can take place in a relatively reflective space without time-sensitive demands for change from administrators or students or faculty. So our plan is to take this moment of piloting and make it a reflective and rhetorical moment both for the department and the program. And so we will ask again the questions of each proposed change that emerges. *What is the adaptive potential of including multilingual texts in a shared set of readings? How does the idea of partnering with writing students and teachers in Mexico align with outcomes for the rhetorical use of technology? How will our criteria for student and teacher success change, and how will we monitor that change together in dialogue?* Reflecting on this, we developed the second element in our heuristic.

Generative Xings Heuristic, Continued

> 2. *Foster individual exploration of positionality within a programmatic vision.* This is continual and continuous work: positionalities and privilege change.

Programmatic Activities and Heuristic

Developing a writing program as an intentionally *designed* entity is not an easy task. Elizabeth Wardle discusses at length the "tangled set of longstanding problems and questions surrounding first-year composition: What should it do? How can it do that? How can well-prepared teachers be appropriately employed to undertake this work? And how can we assess our efforts there?" These issues have "perpetuated systems where writing program administrators" sometimes end up directing writing programs that exist as little more than an organizational topos where "writing program" becomes a collective noun, the umbrella, that signifies the first-year writing sequence. Under this organizational scheme, often there is no/little cohesion between classes. The program itself struggles to have a discernible identity, mission, or vision. Whether a class is successful, whether a class embraces progressive languaging practices and encourages students to explore and experiment with language and questions of how writing and rhetoric *work* in different situations is almost entirely dependent on the instructor and their own experience with languaging and best teaching practices.

The writing program at UTRGV has worked to overcome the tangled set of problems and present students and faculty a writing program informed by writing studies research and practices, including those practices that support "a deep and mindful attending" (Inoue 17) to building transnational spaces.

Our writing program focused its attention on formalizing a programmatic identity, developing curriculum, adjusting hiring practices, and providing challenging professional development. Although these are presented in order, in practice these guiding principles developed simultaneously. That is, while we wrote and approved a mission statement, we also transformed our hiring practices, while we also revisited and revised curriculum. In some ways the simultaneity is beneficial. We did not have to wait until we had a mission statement to figure out what professional development to offer. We did not have to wait until our curriculum was finalized to change our hiring practices. That meant we could do the work of attending to languaging and transnational practices immediately. The disadvantage of a simultaneous process is that there is a lot to attend to. Processes can feel messy or scattered. Faculty can feel overwhelmed by changes and activity. Inoue reminds us, however, that "compassion"—and ensuring a program (its policies, curriculum, faculty, physical spaces, and so on) establishes "a deep and mindful attending" toward its students *is* a *necessary* compassion—"is more than feeling empathy, but a doing something" (Wardle). Despite the busyness, then, we are "doing something."

Writing Program Identity

The writing program identity should be more than the collective personality of all its lecturers. A writing program should have vector (direction and magnitude). The question, though, is how to develop an identity with vector that can enact, embody, demonstrate itself to stakeholders and passersby. Returning to threshold concepts, we are reminded that "writers are socialized, changed, through their writing in new environments, and these changes can have deep implications…[the writers] enact an identity in response to social expectations for who they are and what they should be doing" (Scott 49). This, of course, is important to consider for our students who will respond to and encounter the social expectations of the writing courses they work and learn in. This is also important for the development of a writing program identity and ethos. That is, it is possible that a writing program identity *is* what the writing program articulates for itself. Or, at the very least, it is a place to start. This is particularly advantageous for writing programs that either have no identity or, perhaps, feel that they have a negative identity. That articulation of identity needs to be formalized in program documents, which may mean creating those documents for the first time or revising existing documents. A writing program has policy documents (such as peer observation and annual review), but it also could/should have a mission statement and a vision statement, a website, model syllabuses and project descriptions. A writing program needs to create for itself an artifact-driven footprint because there is a "wisdom in producing public documents as one enactment of this productive theorizing, as one way of materializing the program and bearing witness to the breadth of the activity system it represents—past, present, and future" (Charlton et al. 143). More directly: the language we use to invent and describe our (program) identity and our work is *itself* the work of inventing and legitimizing our (program) identity.

As a practical example, the writing program at UTRGV developed an in-house document called *The WP Works* that describes our student learning objectives, maps the SLOs on to the university's core objectives, articulates the writing program pedagogical philosophy, includes a mission statement and a vision statement, briefly details all the events and initiatives the writing program is responsible for, includes a model syllabus and project descriptions, and includes a recommended reading list for faculty on writing research (it's a big document). It is a good reminder of what the writing program is about, and it serves as a handy artifact for new faculty and interested stakeholders. More important, though, is that by writing everything down, we were able to formalize our philosophy and goals as a writing program. We were able to foreground our commitment to student-centered teaching, developing responsive and engaged classrooms, and supporting students' right to their own language. We were also able to build into the process opportunities to revise and revisit. In fact, without a process to revise our philosophy or objectives, we risk becoming entrenched. The identity of a writing program should necessarily be one of growth, development, and adaptation.

Generative Xings Heuristic, Continued

3. *Formalize programmatic identity.* The language we use to describe and invent our identity is itself the work of legitimizing our programmatic identity.

Hiring Practices

We have been lucky in our ability to hire for the long term and increase our disciplinary expertise. As we were forming the new university, we were able to hire six three-year lecturers. While it decreased the amount of sections we could offer, it moved us from one-year appointments (many of whom had some rhetoric and composition pedagogy classes in their MAs and some of whom had MAs with rhetoric and composition specializations) to three-year appointments with a career ladder that formalized the need for growth and development in writing studies. We were able to hire people who were aligned with a metacognitive writing program and sequence because they wanted to do that kind of work and not just because they wanted a job and preferred to stay at the university. We changed our job ads to emphasize hours in composition pedagogy and we all but eliminated part-time hires to teach one to three sections without the ways or means to practically benefit from professional development as adjuncts working other jobs with other outcomes from local schools and IHEs.

These hires still joined a larger collective of professionals, with a mix of creative writing, literature, and rhetoric and composition degrees and a very diverse understanding of our FYW outcomes. We were pulling people from the two previous university cultures into a singular vision, so cohesion has always been a bit tenuous and remains an active area of/for improvement. There wasn't just a programmatic learning curve because of the goals Colin continued to champion and the goals that Andrew revised. It was a mix of individual learning curves, with some trying to figure out how to be successful in a larger and multi-campus program, some trying to figure out how to put their own stamps on a shared curriculum, and some trying to figure out how to impact larger parts of the university (including emerging interests in undergraduate research, service learning, community engagement, and bilingual coursework). If we thought we were seeing a pattern of articulation unfold for how our praxis of many languages in many contexts would play out in classrooms and teaching materials, it was quickly complicated by several more tenure-track hires and nine more three-year lecturers.

The key, which we continue to develop and think more about as hiring has levelled off, is yearly onboarding. We had to rethink orientation activities to last a year and to work for all of us, new to veteran, to bring more voices into the fold and to make space for all those voices at fall kickoffs, where people in all positions could contribute to monthly *Gravity* meetings (the name of our professional development series) that invited instructors to expose us to old practices that still had value, emerging practices that we should be struggling with, and "alternative" practices that didn't quite match any of the dominant threads of writing studies that had stabilized. This extended onboarding approach takes a great amount of time and energy for everyone involved, and it continues to be a difficult thing to manage across a distributed campus. While we have by no means found a way to consistently manage this complexity, we do have a heuristic for sustaining a culture of crossings. Interestingly, enough, it did not find a solution in either hiring people for their specializations (beyond writing pedagogy) or hiring people for cohorts of like-minded instructors. The promise of having an ESL specialist might lead to an individualized approach to an ENGL 1301 sequence that emphasized L2 reading to the detriment of writing instruction and practice. The idea of having multiple committees looking at service-learning ENGL 1302s might lead to siloing and a tricky erosion of scaffolded assignments into proposals and hyper-specialist public documents.

We're not sure if we fell back on or fell forwards to an approach, but our current process combines (1) clear goals for hiring writing experts, (2) clear pathways to projects and partnerships connected to FYW, and (3) continued dialogues about the practices of feedback and peer review. This plays out in three ways. Hiring committees and the department chair had/have opening conversations about writing expertise in terms of the FYW outcomes. Traditional discussions of ethos, pathos, and logos from applicants did not score as high as difficult discussions of audience, purpose, from, and a variety of concepts articulated in *Naming What We Know*. Opportunities for language diversity in classrooms was of course important to these hiring discussions, but it was even more important to articulate all the opportunities the department had established for partnerships with community literacy centers, high school college-readiness programs, and service partners that were looking for long-term materials development. We even had professional writers with backgrounds in creative writing mentoring PhD students in other departments who were struggling as L2 public writers. After five years, we believe we have a much better ecology mapped for our colleagues so they can compare what they (want to) do in FYW to what they could do with another learning partner, and that allows a productive comparative moment for them. We can't really make anyone understand that FYW is just a beginning and can't expertly do all things for all people, but we can help our colleagues find opportunities for teaching writing and reading and rhetoric in multiple contexts as part of their teaching and service enhancements. And in turn, we can open a dialogue about how FYW can adapt (or not) to the explorations in adult education, college transitions, and service-learning. We can work with the languages and goals that a student arrives with and adapt shared public document assignments to the individual student's drive, language and cultural assets, and educational career goals.

Finally, our discussions of language diversity and global rhetoric found an anchor in the discussion of feedback. Our applicants now have to provide samples of feedback on student writing and a feedback philosophy. This puts conversations about standards and "academic writing" front and center in interviews and in continued professional development on how we teach our students and each other to respond to different discourses and discourse communities as we talk about and through our assignment drafts. Language choice, then, becomes dependent on our continuous focus on the audience, and examples like our remix assignment, which we discuss in the next section, become opportunities to think about three ways to represent an idea and how comparing those public documents makes us rethink language as it works across different forms and goals.

Generative Xings Heuristic, Continued

4. *Hire good people.* Simply, hire the team that is best for the students.

Curriculum

Because full-time lecturers comprise our faculty, we can not and do not have a required common syllabus. Instead, we have a model syllabus and project descriptions with agreed-upon anchor points (certain texts, certain assignments). Faculty build out their own syllabi and projects to align with the model syllabus. Faculty may also use the model documents if they prefer. The model syllabus is aligned with our assessment obligations and our pedagogical philosophy. If faculty develop their documents from the model documents, student artifacts will remain aligned for assessment purposes, and courses will align with our writing program philosophy. The model curriculum is revisited and revised every two years (or sooner).

Treating curriculum this way has several implications. First, faculty are continually discussing curriculum. We do not become entrenched with favorite projects, assignments, or lectures. We invent and reinvent the happenings in the classroom. Second, we do not treat curriculum as "the" answer. It is "an" answer, and we work to stay ahead of the curve. In particular, we understand that the classroom is a dynamic, entangled moment that includes instructors, students, technology, space and place, affect, and so on. What works at UTRGV may not necessarily obtain in other institutions and writing programs. This is more about pedagogy and delivery than threshold concepts or best practices for writing instruction (though we acknowledge the field does not always agree on those concepts). That is, what works for our instructors as they teach revision and feedback in south Texas may not work for instructors in north Texas (or New Mexico, or Kentucky, or Oregon, or...) as *they* teach revision and feedback. What's more, what works for Andrew may not also work for Colin. Some teachers are better at incorporating humor and some are better at creating narratives of/for their courses and, still, others are better at a more austere technique. It is important to discuss and challenge our approaches even among ourselves. We want our classes to be meaningful and productive spaces, whatever that might look like. Third, it means faculty are talking about teaching and writing research often. Although lecturers sometimes get short shrift in the hierarchy of the university, our lecturers (we feel) are some of the most expert and professionalized writing instructors in the field.

Our recommendation is that each institution should find a curriculum that works for their unique ecology, an ecology that specifically takes students into account. At UTRGV we use a *writing about writing* curriculum because we find it to be especially powerful for supporting our languaging practices and developing transnational spaces. Students engage with writing as a subject and an activity. In this way, not only do they employ the language practices that they find meaningful, but they immerse themselves in the issues that surround languaging and learning. The inquiry is student-driven, so students are participating in the content in more authentic ways than a traditional instructor-driven assignment, which is why constantly revising curriculum is valuable to us.

Generative Xings Heuristic, Continued

5. *Develop curriculum.* While classes do not need to be identical (perhaps, should not), there should be anchor points that help develop cohesion across sections and instructors.

Professional Development

A writing program that wants to embrace antiracist pedagogy, support student languaging practices, and develop as an interactive transnational space needs to provide robust professional development. It is difficult for a lecturer with a full teaching load to always keep up to date with what is new, interesting, progressive, provocative within the emerging scholarship. The writing program steps in to help mediate that space. Professional development should be a safe space where instructors can work out their ideas and practices, but that does not mean that professional development is judgment-free. Practices that are not good for students should be ended, and PD is a place where those practices can be determined. In addition to allowing faculty space and place to discuss and practice the skills and knowledge of teaching (providing feedback, leading discussions, how to develop classroom activities), professional development is also an area where crucial disciplinary elements can be discussed, debated, and worked on.

For example, after Asao Inoue's 2019 4Cs keynote, the writing program at UTRGV took action. One faculty member led a reading group on social justice. The end of the semester PD included a talking circle where each member of the writing program took a turn discussing Inoue's address without being interrupted. It was a significant and emotional activity that was necessary for our writing program to experience. Our professional development makes us better scholars and better practitioners.

Generative Xings Heuristic, Continued

6. *Provide professional development.* Then, continue to develop, grow, challenge faculty to confront the interesting and challenging developments in the field.

Conclusion

No *one thing* necessarily results in a conscientious transnational space. Addressing curriculum is important. Refocusing faculty attention is critical. Formalizing languaging practices is fundamental. And yet, on their own, each element is little more than a good intention. Radical and purposeful change, however, is found in the confluence of crossings. For example, a writing program with a growth mindset supports continual and progressive professional development which, in turn, strengthens the programmatic identity. Incorporating hiring practices and a curriculum with a "deep and mindful attending," and a thoughtful, compassionate, transnational, and translingual writing program ought to develop.

What if the "basics" mentioned in *The Chronicle of Higher Education* essays by Teller and Jenkins weren't about standard academic English (or another standardized language), but instead included fundamentals like:

- Students need to language and learn across cultural and language borders, a classroom with conventions *sin fronteras*;

- Students should experiment with content and concepts in spaces that allow for invention, creativity, missteps, trial and error (whatever error may be);

- Students deserve classrooms where fundamentals are challenged and tested;

- Students are worthy of teachers, guides, mentors, facilitators regardless of their entry point into the academy, field, workforce, situation, curiosity, or whichever scenario led them to learning.

These are, perhaps, "basics" we could support: the right to a curious life, and guiding tenets that leave "the possibilities for self-hood" open, boundless. Unashamed. Untamed.

Generative Heuristic for Developing and Networking Individual, Programmatic, and Institutional Spaces of Transnational Work

1. Regularly recognize and explore positionality and privilege through dynamic criteria mapping activities

2. Foster individual exploration of positionality within a programmatic and student-facing vision

3. Formalize programmatic identity with built-in feedback loops for faculty input and inquiry

4. Hire engaged people who want to explore positionality in relation to pedagogy

5. Collaboratively develop curriculum through reviewed anchor texts, assignment sequences, threshold concepts

6. Provide regular professional development that makes positionality a resounding question rather than a thematic supplement

Works Cited

Anzaldúa, Gloria. *Borderlands: The New Mestiza = La Frontera.* San Francisco: Spinsters/Aunt Lute, 1987. Print.

Charlton, Colin., et al. *Genadmin: Theorizing Wpa Identities in the Twenty-First Century.* Anderson, S.C: Parlor Press, 2011. Print.

"Fall 2015 UTRGV Freshman Profile." Office of Strategic Analysis and Institutional Reporting, Data and Reports, UTRGV. https://www.utrgv.edu/sair/_files/documents/entering%20freshmen%20profile%20-%20fall%202020 16_updated5-27.pdf. Accessed April 2, 2020.

"Fall 2019 UTRGV Freshman Profile." Office of Strategic Analysis and Institutional Reporting, Data and Reports, UTRGV, https://www.utrgv.edu/sair/data-reports/fall-2019-entering-freshmen-profile.pdf. Accessed April 2, 2020.

Horner, Bruce., et al. "Language Difference in Writing: Towards a Translingual Approach." *College English* 73.3 (2011): 299-17. Print.

Inoue, Asao B. "How Do We Language So People Stop Killing Each Other, Or What Do We Do about White Language Supremacy?" Keynote Presented at the Annual Meeting of the *Conference on College Composition and Communication.* Pittsburgh, PA: 2019. https://tinyurl.com/4C19ChairAddress

Jenkins, Rob. "We Must Help Students Master Standard English." *The Chronicle of Higher Education*, 10 Apr. 2018. https://www.chronicle.com/article/We-Must-Help-Students-Master/243079.

—. "Why We Must Get Back to Basics in Teaching Composition." *The Chronicle of Higher Education*, 29 Jan. 2020. https://www.chronicle.com/article/Why-We-Must-Get-Back-to-Basics/247918.

Martins, David S., editor. *Transnational Writing Program Administration.* Boulder, CO: UP of Colorado, 2015. Print.

Roozen, Kevin. "Writing Is Linked to Identity." *Naming What We Know: Threshold Concepts of Writing Studies,* edited by Linda Adler-Kassner and Elizabeth Wardle, Utah State UP, 2016, pp. 50-51. Print.

Scott, Tony. "Writing Enacts and Creates Identities and Ideologies." *Naming What We Know: Threshold Concepts of Writing Studies,* edited by Linda Adler-Kassner and Elizabeth Wardle, Utah State UP, 2016, pp. 48-49. Print.

Skinnell, Ryan. *Conceding Composition: A Crooked History of Composition's Institutional Fortunes.* Utah State UP, 2016. Print.

Teller, Joseph R. "Are We Teaching Composition All Wrong?" *The Chronicle of Higher Education,* 03 Oct. 2016. https://www.chronicle.com/article/Are-We-Teaching-Composition/237969.

Wardle, Elizabeth. "Intractable Writing Program Problems, *Kairos,* and Writing about Writing: A Profile of the University of Central Florida's First-Year Composition Program." *Composition Forum,* 27 (2013). https://composition forum.com/issue/27/ucf.php

Williams, Raymond. *Marxism and Literature.* Oxford University Press, 1977. Print.

Chapter 5

All Writers Have More Englishes to Learn: Translingual First-Year Composition Classes' Promotion of Composition's Threshold Concepts

Asmita Ghimire and Elizabethada A. Wright

University of Minnesota Duluth

Abstract: As much recent research illustrates, despite the field of rhetoric and composition's embrace of inclusion, it still omits many translingual and transnational people from its terrain. Not only does the field omit transnational students, as the work of both Bruce Horner and Suresh Canagarajah illustrates, but it also excludes non-native English speaking teachers of writing. For example the work of Ayse Naz Bulamur, Todd Rueker et al., and George Braine reveals how translingual instructors are often discriminated against by students, other faculty, and administrators.

This article focuses on how first-year classes can better open up FYC classes to the values of both translingual faculty and students, and simultaneously enhancing the education of monolingual students, by recognizing how the differences between native and non-native English speakers encourage students comprehension of the "threshold concepts" of composition, as explored by Linda Adler-Kassner, Elizabeth Wardle and the contributors to their book Naming What We Know. Non-native English speaking students and teachers come to their United States classrooms with a variety of backgrounds, and these students and faculty not only have to negotiate language, but they also continually encounter new cultures, challenges, and ways of thinking. To manage, they continually need to respond to changing rhetorical situations, using their critical thinking skills and logical approaches to arguments.

This paper illustrates how a translingual composition classroom, with native and non-native speaking students engaged in such negotiations and encounters through their writing assignments, promotes the five main threshold metaconcepts: 1) writing is an activity and a subject of study, 2) writing speaks to situations through recognizable forms, 3) writing enacts and creates identities and ideologies, 4) all writers have more to learn, and 5) writing is a cognitive ability.

Keywords: translingual, transnational, monolingual, Non-Native English Speaking Teachers (NNEST), Threshold Concepts, Englishes, comparative rhetoric, rhetorical situation, rhetorical attunement

***

Scholars within the field of rhetoric and composition appear to agree that transnationalism needs to be an important component of our classes (e.g., CCCC), yet outside the consensus many scholars express concern that First-Year Composition (FYC) is approaching transnationalism superficially (e.g., Hesford et al.). For example, international perspectives are relegated to the margins of the curriculum, offering pseudo-internationalism from a solely North American perspective. Most myopic perhaps is the trouble FYC classes seem to have discarding a monolingual standard or examining how normalized Western sematic practice stems from particular socio-cultural and historic situations.

The university's attitude toward non-native English speaking teachers (NNEST) of writing illustrates FYC's problem with transnationalism. Because of the academy's implicit assumptions that United States students speak and/or need a monolingual standard of written English (SWE), international teaching assistants in FYC who are NNEST are relegated to ESL sections or prohibited from teaching FYC in the first place.

We are well acquainted with this limitation. One of us (Asmita) came as a graduate teaching assistant (GTA) to the United States from Nepal with 23-years of spoken English in school, a master's degree in English, and a desire to learn more about rhetoric from a North American perspective; the other of us (Liz) is a monolingual tenured professor of writing. Despite her acceptance at the university and invitation to the role of GTA, Asmita found even before she arrived that one university administrator had hesitations about her role as a GTA, and when Asmita took the rather subjective university oral test for international students, she did not "pass." Fortunately, Asmita was able to remain, though she was a "Teacher of Record" as were other GTAs. Working together in a graduate class, we immediately began exploring the issue of transnationalism and translingualism as Asmita wrote papers that introduced Liz to the importance of this perspective.

This chapter comes from this rhetorical situation and resulting partnership. Recognizing that seasoned North American teachers have much to learn from NNEST of writing, we first overview the scholarship regarding transnationalism in U.S. writing classes. We next present a model curriculum for FYC that puts NNEST at the forefront of FYC classes, so that NNESTs can instruct both students and native English speaking teachers on how to bring a transnational perspective to students with both mono—and multi-cultural perspectives. This curriculum illustrates that awareness and acceptance of Englishes in the FYC classes requires the comprehension of transnational practices: American SWE is one variety of English.

Recognizing that many instructors might be hesitant to embrace such a curriculum, feeling it might sacrifice the traditionally "important" elements of the assumed monolingual class, we then illustrate how this curriculum brings to students ways of thinking about writing that exemplify the threshold concepts of rhetoric and composition articulated in Linda Adler-Kassner and Elizabeth Wardle's text, *Naming What We Know*.

One caveat though: because of the situation in which both of us exist, we have not had the opportunity to explore this curriculum in practice. We have thought about the curriculum, read about others' curriculum, and discussed the concepts with others, but we have yet to put it into practice. Therefore, what we present is a theoretical perspective that has been produced out of our experiences and study within this field. We are looking forward to putting it into practice—or hearing from others who put it into practice.

Everyone's English is alien

In 2006, Paul Kei Matsuda persuasively argued that despite the "myth of linguistic homogeneity" regarding students in the U.S., most of our students are multilingual—and much quantitative data supports his assertion (e.g., Canagarajah, "The Place"; Bizzell; Kachru; Horner, "Introduction: Cross"). In fact, David Graddol has shown that native speakers of English lost their majority in the United States in the 1970s, and H.G. Widdowson presents statistics that argue the Anglo-elite no longer "own" English. What exists now in most U.S. classes is a multitude of Englishes, not solely the one associated with SWE, and scholars such as Donahue as well as Horner and Tetreault argue that instructors cannot take a singular English for granted. Increasingly, students will encounter Asian, European, African, South American, and indigenous Englishes within their classes, their careers, and their civic lives—and within these Englishes exist a multitude of variations.

As Suresh H. Canagarajah argues ("The Place"), the U.S. classroom's absence of awareness of Englishes comes from many locations. Tom Fox claims the myth of the United States' monolingualism results from "a violent process of unification that involved homogeneity, centralization, and standardization" (16). Matsuda argues the myth has been perpetuated by policies of containment that treat multilingualism as a problem that needs to be remedied. Nonetheless, U.S. school structures have been built on the myth of linguistic homogeneity (Horner and Trimbur, Kaplan), and SWE has been treated as the target for all students—especially in FYC classes (Canagarajah, "Place"; Trimbur; Lu and Horner). As Wendy Hesford et al., Tardy, and Lalicker observe, this target is ironic, not only because it is based upon inaccurate assumptions, but because the universities are increasingly trying to promote their internationalism—yet this internationalism seems to be preserved for privileged white students who can afford the opportunity to study abroad.

The treatment of NNEST is indicative of the problem with the U.S. university's adherence to these myths and its lack of transnationalism. Scholars such as Ayse Naz Bulamur have detailed some of the discriminatory practices NNEST have experienced in and out of the classroom. George Braine's comparative analyses of NNEST from Northern Europe and other countries suggest that the negativity toward NNEST results not from their knowledge or even their accents, but from long-standing prejudices of race and ethnicity. And repeatedly, scholars observe that when NNEST of writing do teach, they are usually relegated to ESL classes, continuing what Matsuda terms the culture of containment.

However, despite the common beliefs that international students do not have much to contribute to the classroom (Hesford et al.), much research suggests there is enormous gain to be had from their perspective. As Canagarajah notes, the future of English lies in the plural English. Observing that there are as many experts in Sri Lankan English as there are in American English, Canagarajah ("The Place") questions the meaning of the term "native" speaker of English, and with many other scholars (e.g., Swales) he predicts that in the future all English speakers will need to be proficient in multiple Englishes and have to learn how to adapt to those they are unfamiliar with.

This need, however, does not mean that monolingual U.S. students in FYC classes will be losing out. In fact, much suggests that by embracing multilingual Englishes and a transnational perspective, all FYC students in the United States can benefit. For example, Christiane Donahue comments that students who not comfortable in transnational and translingual contexts will be disadvantaged in the future, and John M. Swales argues, with globalization students need to be broadly rather than narrowly English proficient (56-57), a perspective much echoed (e.g., Jordan; Kaplan; Canagarajah, "The Place";

Hesford et al.). Thus, as Gallagher and Noonan state, our goal is not to lower standards, but to rethink them (164).

Certainly, the task of considering the transnationality of these contexts is not easy; it will, as Donahue observes, "denaturalize" the language and contexts in which students feel comfortable. However, such denaturalizing can benefit students as it calls "attention to the material cost to speakers who have to submit, around the world, to a particular English" as it also teaches students to listen "to the logic of 'alien' Englishes" (Hesford et al. 226).

The curriculum suggested below does just that: denaturalizes *everyone's* English as it frames *everyone's* English as "alien" and asks people to suspend judgement and recognize the logic of the "alien." With this egalitarianism in its denaturalization, this curriculum also puts the international teacher, the NNEST of writing, at the forefront, since this individual is more familiar with the kind of negotiation the curriculum asks for than is the monolingual instructor. Additionally, the NNEST can help the monolingual teacher initiate the suggested curriculum. Additionally, this curriculum posits that a transnational perspective is essential to understand Englishes. Instead of memorizing differences in rhetorical and linguistic structures, this approach facilitates students' understandings of situations in various cultures that create the contexts from which the variety of Englishes evolve.

A Means for NNEST of Writing to Lead the Curriculum

In her examination of the English academic writing competence of Turkish students in Turkey, Louisa Buckingham observes the many ways she perceived these students as having disadvantages as they compose in English. Such a study might appear to delegitimize the curriculum we propose; after all, asking disadvantaged students to lead FYC lessons might not seem advantageous. Yet a second aspect of Buckingham's observations offers a perspective that presents the students as advantaged: these Turkish students were both aware of their limitations and regularly used rhetorical and linguistic strategies to overcome their limitations and disadvantages.

It is because of multilinguistic instructors' similarly developed awarenesses and strategies that NNEST of writing are not only best suited to lead the curriculum we suggest, but they can facilitate monolingual instructors with the curriculum since, too often, monolingual instructors do not know their own limitations nor use linguistic strategies to communicate with speakers of other Englishes.

Too much pedagogy in FYC classes across the nation others transnational students. The status quo does not see where and how the U.S. curriculum needs to fit in with the Englishes of the world, instead of the other way around

(Donahue; Lalicker). Similarly, too often monolingual instructors of FYC do not recognize the many resources available via our transnational GTAs and students. With the approach we are advocating, all involved individuals work with Englishes and cultures with which they are not familiar. In this more equitable exchange, transnational GTAs are advantaged because the situation with multiple languages and cultures is one with which they are familiar.

To be explicit, the objectives of this pedagogy are to help students

- Gain experiences that will allow them to cross various learning thresholds

- Recognize that "differences" in writing often occur because of varying cultural perspectives

- Develop strategies to understand and communicate effectively within various "Englishes"

We are not suggesting this pedagogy without building on precedents: in fact, we echo in many ways the curricula and pedagogical goals of William Lalicker and Patricia Bizzell, and we note suggestions from Horner, NeCamp, and Donahue while taking advice from Horner and Trimbur as well as Horner alone. Skeptics should recognize that, like Bizzell, our first pedagogical goal is to help students improve their abilities to read and write (137). However, also like Bizzell, we introduce a transnational perspective to challenge the notion of what is correct and elegant writing. While FYC classes have been increasingly noting, as does Northeastern University's 2011 Writing Center mission statement, "'effective writing' must be defined in the contexts of writers' goals, audiences' expectation, and situational factors such as available technologies" (qtd. Gallagher and Noonan 164), the transnational has been missing from what United States classrooms explore with writers and audiences. As a result, we in the U.S. exclude much, as we are blind to our own omissions. As Donahue comments, "We must recognize that U.S. framings are always culturally, geographically, and historically located and loaded" (232).

Two sample assignments

Assignment one

The first assignment is similar to one proposed by Jay Jordan, asking students to write informally about their experiences with transnationalism and translingualism. While international students might find the examples of experiences easy to locate, white middle-class North American students might find the task more difficult. Instructors could encourage these students' encounters with people they didn't understand or whose cultures seemed "different." Similarly, these students could be encouraged to think about current events, popular culture, and even culinary experiences. From this first assignment, students would be asked to write an essay for a class journal regarding the benefits of transnationalism, taking a stance as to how transnationalism can or cannot be beneficial.

Students would then be asked to share their assignments, both the first and second, with others, discussing the differences in experiences as well as within the construction of prose, creation of evidence, organization, etc. Following Jordan's advice of suspending judgement of others' writing, the instructor would ask students to comment on areas in which they find the approach unfamiliar. For example, instead of noting a grammatical error, students would comment on how the construction of the sentence is different from how they might have constructed it. Instead of stating that the essay needs a thesis, students would comment that they have been taught to state the main point of their argument early in the text. Instead of stating that the evidence for a claim does not seem sufficient, the student would ask why further support was not added.

Inviting students to consider the logic of "Englishes" can help students rhetorically analyze the role of content, structure, lexis, syntax, and semantics in particular local textual situations. It can help students to see how certain forms of English are networked within a larger context, creating intersectionality within the outer world. As language is not outside of politics and culture, the use of language and writing in diverse social situations is not isolated from the ideology, politics and cultural context. Inviting students to engage in these practices can help them gain the skills of "rhetorical attunement" or "shuttling" that Rebecca Lorimer Leonard and Canagarajah ("The Place") have discussed NNEST as possessing. Such abilities allow the writer to have an "ear for, or tuning toward, difference or multiplicity" (Leonard 228). This negotiating ability can not only make the multilingual writer aware of the particular situations and how to make conscious appropriate choices, but may also assist the monolingual writer in the United States become more attuned with other larger cultural issues.

Comparative rhetoric examines many of these multiplicities. One of the most well-known discussions of these differences makes clear the reality of Canagarajah's observation that "not every instance of nonstandard usage by a student is an unwitting error" ("The Place" 609). Writing about the use of the phrase "can able to" by a Chinese student from Malaysia, Min-Zhan Lu explains that the student uses the phrase intentionally: since "can" and "able to" have different meanings in the student's first language, the student put them together to stress the ability to do something even with both environmental and community restraints ("Professing"; Canagarajah, "The Place"). Similarly, Lu points out the logic of the phrase used in Beijing "collecting money toilets" (21-22) and Widdowson the word "prepone" as the opposite of "postpone." George Mason University's *Valuing Written Accents* observes that one Indian student's use of the idiom "my house is coming," to mean "I am getting closer to my house," is a perfectly acceptable English phrase in India, translated literally from the Hindi (21). For many Indian students who are native English speakers, such an English phrase is perfectly acceptable. *Valuing Written Accents* notes many such grammatically acceptable usages in other Englishes that stem from differences in language and culture: with many Asian languages not using article or tenses, their usages appear irrelevant to many Asian NNES.

In addition to sentence-level ones, there are other areas in which students might also observe differences. For example, Weiguo Qu notes the many ways in which the Chinese tradition of argumentation differs enormously from the West's. While the Western tradition of argument works to resolve uncertainty, the Chinese tradition "presupposes some certainty before the argument even starts. That is to say, the main business of argument is not to prove but to expound on a certainty" (71). Additionally, the concepts of correctness, clarity, and originality differ in meaning in China from the U.S.'s meaning. Similarly, Kaplan comments on how many Asian cultures treat what counts as authority, evidence, or acceptable sources differently than do Western cultures (x-xii). Canagarajah's detailed discussion of a paper published by the Sri Lankan member of the Jaffna Tamil Society illustrates how article introductions, statements of claims, structures, constructions of ethos, and so forth differ dramatically from papers published in Western journals ("Toward a Writing" 592-3). Canagarajah notes that much of this difference stems from the differences in expectations of academics. Instead of expecting its scholar to publish, this culture values "the oral construction of knowledge" and expects scholars to adopt what Canagarajah terms "a civic ethos": "Scholars must show what important service they are performing for their community by writing this paper and/or constructing this knowledge" (592). Though Robert Kaplan's 1966 concepts of difference in thinking in various cultures might be outdated, he was correct in observing the difference in various countries' cognitive approaches to communication.

One of the most significant differences in approaches to writing is one rarely considered by the U.S. field of Rhetoric and Composition: while some cultures (such as the United States) assume writer responsibility for clarity, others assume "reader responsibility" for interpretation of meaning. As Donahue observes, our field and classrooms little explore the notions of linguistic transparency (228), a notion that comes into conflict with these two interpretations of responsibility. While many scholars and classrooms in the United States assume the superiority of the Western way of doing communication, the transnationalism of the world and cultures that believe in the relevance of their ways of doing things suggests people in the United States start understanding why alternative approaches have validity.

Measuring Success

The assessment goals for this assignment should be considering whether students are able to:

- Identify elements of another student's writing that are inconsistent with the identifying student's norms

- Provide a logical and culturally sensitive explanation of why the other student created text inconsistent with the identifying student's norms (e.g., explanations similar to Lu's or *Valuing Written Accents'*)

Assignment two

The next part of this proposed curriculum involves asking students to write a research paper in which they integrate what they have learned about transnationalism from various sources and each other. As students observe these differences and/or many others, they may chart them for their third assignment as they combine these observations with research. One of the requirements for this research paper would be that students look for sources outside of those from North America or the United Kingdom. As many proponents of transnationalism observe, scholars of rhetoric and composition in North America rarely venture out of the continent for sources. Even one of the most noted scholars of transnationalism, Bruce Horner, has noted his own lack in this area ("Toward a Writing"). In an article with Necamp and Donovan, the three scholars explore how Horner could have strengthened his earlier arguments if he had gone beyond North America. Writing alone, Donahue observes the length of time it took for Bakhtin's scholarship to be translated into English, asking how rhetoric and composition scholars feel about the fact that "the most appropriate theory" for them could be "untranslated into English" (227).

Students could get further experience with the differences in Englishes by exploring journals written in Englishes, but written for journals and books published outside the usually explored countries. This exploration of these journals from outside the United States would further establish for monolingual students that the differences between their sentence constructions and that of multilingual students are not errors, but choices based on cultural situations. While such journals might at first seem difficult to access, internet searches can quickly provide such sources. When we were considering this assignment and intrigued by Canagarajah's discussion of Sri Lankan academic texts, we quickly found the link https://www.sljol.info/site/ journals/hosted/ that lists 86 Sri Lankan academic journals for various disciplines.

The problem, though, is how to approach asking students to compose the results of this assignment. As Wardle has compellingly argued, the traditional "mutt genre" research paper (a genre created in writing classes with an audience of the instructor that students will never be replicated outside of academic classes) serves little purpose to any writing class, let alone one focusing on transnational rhetorical situations.

Instead, something more along the lines of bringing in the "funk" as Heather Bastian suggests or creating an assemblage such as that proposed by Jennifer Wingard might better serve the curriculum of this transnational class. Providing the instructions for the assignment within the genre of game instructions, Bastian creates an assignment asking students to analyze the genre of a text using another genre to create the analysis—however, the assignment requests students not engage in the traditional essay, since, as Bastian posits, what students will be writing in their future lives no one is sure. The assignment for Bastian's class fits the logic of this transnational curriculum, asking them to think critically while gauging appropriateness. Within this transnational class, students might similarly play with genres. Recognizing how genres differ from culture to culture, they might take their second assignment's essay for the class journal using a genre and style more appropriate for a culture with which the student was not familiar before the class.

In another "funk" type assignment, Wingard asks students in her Houston classroom to examine their city and their role within it. The product Wingard asks her students to create is an assemblage, bringing "together texts which are seemingly distant from one another, yet through contiguous reading it becomes clear that there are certain ideologies and material realities that join them together" (565). The goal, then, of the assemblage is to join seemingly unrelated discursive materials in interactions that allow audiences to reconceptualize interactions (566). What Wingard finds is that students engage in their own histories within Houston, assembling these histories with other histories, stories, and statistics. Similarly, this transnational class might build on their own histories of transnationalism with artifacts of transnationalism or myths of monolingualism that surround them.

Yet another assignment for this final, "research paper," assignment would be to have the students find an international journal that would be appropriate for their essay and write for that journal. For example, exploring Sri Lankan journals, we found the *Sabaragamuwa University Journal*, whose focus is to provide a "forum for Sri Lankan and international scholars to publish good quality articles on original academic research as well as on innovative teaching practices." Writing for such a journal and possibly exploring others, students would hopefully begin to see how both disciplines and cultures shape the generic conventions that they too often accept as de facto realities.

The fourth and final assignment for this curriculum is a repeat of the first: a reflection on the student's experience with transnationalism. The curriculum of this transnational FYC class will have altered the students' actual experiences, and hopefully made them reconsider how rhetorical and linguist conventions work.

Measuring Success

The assessment goals for this final assignment should be considering whether students are able to

- Cite and utilize sources in English from non-North American or British journals

- Identify the genre that the student chooses to write their assignments in

- Articulate the action that the student's genre attempts to achieve and how the genre's form is shaped to achieve that action

- Create text that meets the appropriate form and seeks to achieve the action of the genre

Crossing Thresholds

All this curriculum might appear ideal and wonderful; however, with the many tasks that must be accomplished in the FYC class, there is only so much time to teach students. Some people might ask: while instructors are trying to teach students how to write, how can they engage in such transnational lessons?

Yet the issue of what we should teach in FYC has been the subject of study beyond discussions of transnationalism. While some textbooks still expound on grammatical correctness, structures of introductions and conclusions, and even outlining formats and while English language advanced placement tests stress the primacy of thesis statements, a body of rhetoric and composition scholars has been discussing what kind of thinking FYC need to promote. Building on the field of economics' idea of "threshold concepts," the thinking a person needs to inherently embrace to master their field, Adler-Kassner and Wardle have collaborated with other scholars to determine what kind of thinking rhetoric and composition classes need to promote.

Instead of suggesting pedagogies of correctness, structure, outlining, or thesis creation, these rhetoricians have articulated five main threshold metaconcepts, though they note this work in still being developed: 1) writing is an activity and a subject of study, 2) writing speaks to situations through recognizable forms, 3) writing enacts and creates identities and ideologies, 4) all writers have more to learn, and 5) writing is a cognitive ability. The transnational curriculum we have created can help students embrace each of these metaconcepts.

It is important, though, to recognize that these threshold metaconcepts are not elements that should be explicated taught in a classroom or "assessed." Instead, they are concepts that instructors should always consider when they are creating assignments or developing assessment measures. As Adler-Kassner and Wardle write,

> There is a difference between naming and describing principles and practices that extend from the research base of a discipline...and stripping the complexity from these principles in order to distill them into convenient categories to which generic attributes can be associated or attached. Any attempt to create a "learning checklist" with these...threshold concepts would, in fact, engage in this complexity stripping....
>
> Rather than becoming concerned with creating threshold concepts assignments of stripped-down threshold concepts checklists, teachers might more productively consider which threshold concepts inform (or should inform) their classes...and whether their curricula and activities are productively acting out of and introducing students to those threshold concepts. (8-9)

Thus, as we suggest the above assignments and assessment, and as we briefly discuss the threshold concepts for rhetoric and composition below, we are not creating a checklist for these concepts. Instead, we are attempting are using the concepts, recognizing how much NNEST of writing have to contribute, to inform the creation of the assignments.

Writing is a social and rhetorical activity

Too often, students in classes that assume monolinguistic homogeneity also assume claims and evidence are stable. They don't recognize the fluidity of what can be claimed or used as evidence: everyone they know believes certain tenets; therefore, the tenets are stable and there is no need to "create" ideas. However, as Kevin Roozen writes in Adler-Kassner and Wardle's collection, students need to recognize that writing "is always an attempt to address the needs of an audience."

If teachers can help students consider their potential audiences and purposes, they can better help them understand what makes a text effective or not, what it accomplishes, and what it falls short of accomplishing (18). Asking students to denaturalize their assumptions about most aspects of writing as they recognize how different cultures have different expectations forces students to consider who the audience is and what can make that audience find the text effective and accomplish its goals. Beginning to recognize different cultures' assumptions regarding reader—or writer-responsible texts allows students to recognize what Charles Bazerman and David Russell write of regarding the troublesome nature of readers and writers sharing and mediating meaning (22).

Writing speaks to situations through recognizable forms

As students begin to recognize how linguistic and rhetorical structures change with transnational situatedness, they can increasingly recognize how effective texts are results of human action. Although most students in mononational classes may enter classes believing language and rhetorical forms are stable, exploration of transnational texts will encourage them to see that all texts are like genres in that they are "habitual responses to recurring socially bounded situations" (Hart-Davidson 39). North America's focus on thesis statements announcing texts' purposes early in texts are responses to the recurring situations focusing on efficiency. Asia's focus on texts that ask readers to consider various meanings are responses to recurring situations focusing on situational ambiguity.

Just as Carolyn Miller observes that genre does more than create forms but creates the forms in response to reoccurring situations, texts of various cultures exist as more than structures, but have been structured in response to the cultures' reoccurring situations. With students noting the relationships between the differences and these situations, students will begin to develop the awarenesses that Buckingham observes in the Turkish students as they attempt to communicate in English.

Writing enacts and creates identities and ideologies

One of the more tantalizing aspects of the suggested curriculum is its denaturalization process. In asking students to write for journals published outside North America and the UK, mononational students may resist and insist that their accustomed formatting, genres, and linguistic structures are superior. In asking students to let these customs go, these students may find their identities and ideologies challenged. Such a situation replicated for the mononational student is what transnational students encounter repeatedly in the United States.

In suspending judgment, all students will hopefully achieve what Roozen writes of the third threshold metaconcept: that writing "functions as a key form of socialization" and 'that the difficulties people have with writing are not necessarily due to a lack of intelligence or a diminished level of literacy but rather to whether they can see themselves as participants in a particular community" (51).

This transnational class is difficult because it asks students to rethink and challenge their accepted norms as students recognize the identity and ideological politics of rhetoric. As Kathleen Blake Yancey notes, students have engaged in a "lifelong process of balancing individual perspectives and processes with the opportunities, demands, constraints, and genres of specific rhetorical situations and contexts of the larger culture" (52). This curriculum then unbalances the perspectives and processes introducing rhetorical situations and contexts of different cultures.

All writers have more to learn and writing is (also always) a cognitive ability

In Liz's experience as a Writing Program Administrator, she often faced students who wanted to be exempt from FYC classes because they had "already taken the class in high school." She was repeatedly assured by these students that they knew all they needed to know about FYC. Eventually, Liz began recognizing that this statement itself was evidence that these appealing students needed the class: clearly they had not embraced the fourth of the threshold concepts. On the other hand, graduate students—like Asmita—repeatedly recognized how little they knew—despite years of and degrees illustrating vast knowledge and experience.

Working with this curriculum and denaturalizing assumptions about writing can make students recognize how much they don't know. The assumptions of what is effective in a text can be shattered when a person begins to write in a transnational perspective. Certainly, such denaturalization forces students to break out of habitual writing tendencies, or as Chris Anson expresses it, to break out of "entrenched" practices. Such learning is difficult. Failure can occur when writing for cultures one is unfamiliar with; however, as all the scholars in Adler-Kassner and Wardle's collection write, failure, revision, and hard work helps writers grow.

Similarly, reflection on these experiences will make students more aware of the complexness of language—and how much more they have to learn.

***

As we stated in our introduction, we have not had the opportunity to put this curriculum into practice. Administrative restrictions on our time and curriculum have made all the proposals we have here theoretical. However, this curriculum illustrates the three-fold response to transnationalism that Hesford et al. desire (120): it examines the multiplicity of identity positions and addresses many of the challenges NNEST of writing face. Perhaps most importantly, it is a curriculum that is "comparative, cross-cultural, and enables transnational explorations which prompts students to understand the value and significance of diversity and relationality in an era of globalization" (12).

We state that we have not experienced the curriculum ourselves, yet that is not entirely true. Liz now thinks about how differences in rhetoric and language result from cultural differences, and she has begun to explore reading and publishing beyond North America and the UK. No longer does she encourage students to adopt American English at the sacrifice of their own. Instead, she is trying to better understand the situations of Nepal and many other countries that make various Englishes what they are—and she knows she and her monolingual students will need to know more of these Englishes in the future. Asmita has continued recognizing how she must adapt her textual conventions as she continues her education in the United States. However, she has also recognized that she is not the only one receiving knowledge; she has much to give monocultural students and faculty she meets and teaches.

We teach and learn every day.

Works Cited

Adler-Kassner, Linda., and Elizabeth Wardle. *Naming What We Know: Threshold Concepts of Writing Studies.* Utah State University Press, 2015.

Anson, Chris. "Habituated Practice Can Lead to Entrenchment." *Naming What We Know: Threshold Concepts of Writing Studies.* edited by Adler-Kassner and Wardle, Utah State University Press, 2015, pp. 77-78.

Bastian, Heather. "Students' Affective Response to "Bringing the Funk" in the First Year Classroom. *CCC,* Vol. 69, No. 1, 2017, pp. 6-24.

Bazerman, Charles. "Writing Expresses and Shares Meaning to Be Reconstructed by the Reader." *Naming What We Know: Threshold Concepts of Writing Studies.* edited by Adler-Kassner and Wardle, Utah State University Press, 2015, pp. 21-23.

Bizzell, Patricia. "Toward 'Transcultural Literacy' at a Liberal Arts College." *Reworking English in Rhetoric and Composition: Global Interrogations, Local*

Interventions, edited by Bruce Horner and Karen Kopelson, SIUP, 2014, pp. 131-74.

Braine, George. "A history of research on non-native English speaking teachers." *Non-Native Language Teachers: Perceptions, Challenges, and Contributions to the Profession*, edited by Enric Llurda, Springer, 2005, pp. 13-24.

Buckingham, Louisa. "Development of English Academic Writing Competence by Turkish Scholars." *International Journal of Doctoral Studies*, Vol. 3, 2008, pp. 1-18. *Ebscohost*.

Bulamur, Ayse Naz. "Legitimacy of Teaching English Composition as a Non-Native Speaker." *Universal Journal of Educational Research*, vol.1, no.3, 2013, pp. 170-174.

Canagarajah, A. Suresh. "The Place of World Englishes in Composition: Pluralization Continued." *CCC*, Vol. 57, No. 4, 2006, pp. 586-619.

—. "Toward a Writing Pedagogy of Shuttling between Languages: Learning from Multilingual Writers." *College English*, Vol 68, No. 6, 2006, pp. 589-604.

"CCCC Statement on Globalization in Writing Studies Pedagogy and Research." *Conference on College Composition and Communication*, 16 June 2018. cccc.ncte.org/cccc/resources/positions/globalization.

Donahue, Christiane. "'Internationalization' and Composition Studies: Reorienting the Discourse." *CCC*, Vol. 61, No. 2, 2009, pp. 212-243.

Fox, Tom. "Standards and Purity: Understanding Institutional Strategies to Insure Homogeneity." *The Writing Program Interrupted: Making Space for Critical Discourse*, edited by Donna Strickland and Jeanne Gunner. Boynton/Cook, 2009, 14-27.

Gallagher, Chris., and Matt Noonan. "Becoming Global: Learning to 'Do' Translingualism." *Crossing Divides: Exploring Translingual Writing Pedagogies and Programs*, edited by Bruce Horner and Laura Tetreault. Utah State UP, 2017, pp. 161-177.

Graddol, David. "The Decline of the Native Speaker." *AILA Review*, Vol. 13, 1999, pp. 57-68.

Hart-Davidson, Bill. "Genres are Enacted by Writers and Readers." *Naming What We Know: Threshold Concepts of Writing Studies*. edited by Adler-Kassner and Wardle, Utah State University Press, 2015, pp. 39-40.

Hesford, Wendy., et al. "Laboring to Globalize a First-Year Writing Program." *The Writing Program Interrupted: Making Space for Critical Discourse*, edited by Donna Strickland and Jeanne Gunner. Boynton/Cook, 2009, pp. 113-125.

Horner, Bruce. "Introduction: Cross-Language Relations in Composition." *College English*, Vol. 68, No. 6, 2006, pp. 569-574. jstor.org/stable/25472175.

—. "Introduction." *Reworking English in Rhetoric and Composition: Global Interrogations, Local Interventions*, edited by Bruce Horner and Karen Kopelson, SIUP, 2014, pp. 1-10.

—. "Teaching Translingual Agency in Iteration: Rewriting Difference." Crossing Divides: Exploring Translingual Writing Pedagogies and Programs, edited by Bruce Horner and Laura Tetreault. Utah State UP, 2017, pp. 87-97.

Horner, Bruce., et al. "Toward a Multilingual Composition Scholarship: From English Only to a Translingual Norm." *CCC*, Vol. 63, No. 2, 2011, pp. 269-300.

Horner, Bruce., and Laura Tetreault. "Introduction." *Crossing Divides: Exploring Translingual Writing Pedagogies and Programs*, edited by Bruce Horner and Laura Tetreault. Utah State UP, 2017, pp. 1-16.

Jordan, Jay. *Redesigning Composition for Multilingual Realities*. NCTE, 2012.

Kaplan, Robert B. "Cultural-thought patterns in inter-cultural education." *Language Learning*, Vol. 16, 1966, pp. 1-20.

—. "Foreword: What in the World is Contrastive Rhetoric." *Contrastive Rhetoric Revisited and Redefined*, edited by Clayann Gilliam Panetta, Erlbaum, 2001, pp. vii-ix.

Kachru, Braj B. "Introduction: The Other Side of English and the 1990s." *The Other Tongue: English across Cultures*, edited by Kachru. University of Illinois Press, 1992, pp. 1-15.

Lalicker, William B. "Enacting Translingual Writing Pedagogy: Structures and Challenges for Two Courses in Two Countries." *Crossing Divides: Exploring Translingual Writing Pedagogies and Programs*, edited by Bruce Horner and Laura Tetreault. Utah State UP, 2017, pp. 51-69.

Leonard, Rebecca Lorimer. "Multilingual Writing as Rhetorical Attunement." *College English*, Vol. 76, No. 3, 2014, pp. 227-247.

Lu, Min-Zhan. "An Essay on the Work of Composition." CCC, Vol. 56, No. 1, 2004, pp. 16-50. *Jstor*.

—. "Professing Multiculturalism: The Politics of Style in the Contact Zone." *CCC*, Vol. 45, No. 4, 1994, 442-58. Jstor.

Lu, Min-Zhan., and Bruce Horner. "Translingual Literacy, Language Difference and Matter of Agency". *College English*, vol.75, no.6, 2013, pp. 582-607.

Matsuda, Paul Kei. "The Myth of Linguistic Homogeneity in U.S. College Composition." *College English*, Vol. 68, No. 6, 2006, pp. 637-651.

Miller, Carolyn. "Genre as Social Action." *Quarterly Journal of Speech*. Vol. 70, No. 2, 1984, pp. 151-167. *Ebscohost*.

Qu, Weiguo. "Critical Literacy and Writing in English: Teaching English in a Cross-Cultural Context." *Reworking English in Rhetoric and Composition: Global Interrogations, Local Interventions*, edited by Bruce Horner and Karen Kopelson, SIUP, 2014. pp. 64-74.

Roozen, Kevin. "Texts Get Their Meaning from Other Texts." *Naming What We Know: Threshold Concepts of Writing Studies*. edited by Adler-Kassner and Wardle, Utah State University Press, 2015, pp. 44-47.

—. "Writing is A Social and Rhetorical Activity." *Naming What We Know: Threshold Concepts of Writing Studies*. edited by Adler-Kassner and Wardle, Utah State University Press, 2015, pp. 17-19.

Russell, David. "Writing Mediates Activity." *Naming What We Know: Threshold Concepts of Writing Studies*. edited by Adler-Kassner and Wardle, Utah State University Press, 2015, pp. 26-27.

Sabaragamuwa University Journal. http://suslj.sljol.info/about/. Accessed 13 Nov. 2020.

Swales, John M. *Research Genres: Explorations and Applications*. Cambridge UP, 2004.

Tardy, Christine M. "Crossing, or Creating, Divides? A Plea for Transdisciplinary Scholarship." *Crossing Divides: Exploring Translingual Writing Pedagogies and*

Programs. Ed. Bruce Horner and Laura Tetreault. Utah State UP, 2017. pp. 181-189.

Trimbur, John. "Linguistic Memory and the Politics of U.S. English." *College English,* Vol. 68, No. 6, 2006, pp. 575-588.

Valuing Written Accents: Non-native students talk about identity, academic writing, and meeting teachers' expectations. George Mason University. 2nd edition. writtenaccents.gmu.ed.

Widdowson, H.G. "The Ownership of English." *TESOL Quarterly,* Vol. 28, No. 2, 1994, pp. 377-389.

Wingard, Jennifer. "Assembling Houston: Writing and Teaching the Neoliberal City." *JAC,* Vol. 33, No. 3-4, pp. 553-583. http://www.jaconlinejournal.com/archives/vol33.3/7Dingo.pdf

Yancey, Kathleen Blake. "Learning to Write Effectively Requires Different Kinds of Practice, Time, and Effort." *Naming What We Know: Threshold Concepts of Writing Studies.* edited by Adler-Kassner and Wardle, Utah State University Press, 2015, pp. 64-66.

Chapter 6

Translingual and Transnational Pedagogies Enacted: Linguistic and Cultural Trajectory Narratives in First-Year Composition

Demet Yigitbilek

Illinois State University

Abstract: In light of the changing demographics and linguistic realities of educational contexts, it is no longer the case that students in US college composition classrooms are native-speakers of English, though mostly considered to be so by default (Matsuda, 2006). As a result, in the era of post-monolingualism (Yildiz, 2012), FYC programs are transnational spaces and it is necessary to adapt to these changes. Therefore, in such a diverse landscape, how writing instructors respond to and enact translingual and transnational pedagogies becomes highly important.

To this end, drawing from the growing body of research in translingualism (Motha, et al., Canagarajah, Ayash) and writing program ecologies (Reiff et al.), as a writing instructor in a predominantly white and monolingual midwestern university, I design and teach FYC courses around the themes of language and cultural diversity. The frameworks embraced and utilized in our award-winning WP build on rhetorical genre studies, cultural-historical activity theory, and translingualism. In that sense, both in the WP and the English department, the whole ecology allows writing instructors to design our courses around the nine learning outcomes, two of which specifically focus on cultural and linguistic diversity in writing (Cultures and Communities: Culturally responsive and ethical representations in writing; and Translingual and transnational literacies: Attention to diverse language practices).

In this chapter, I present a unit plan on cultural and linguistic diversity in writing, along with the materials and tools I use and the writing prompts I provide students with to increase their awareness of linguistic diversity and how culture, along with other identity aspects and individual factors, influence one's literate activities. I end the unit with a major project of linguistic trajectory narrative in which they look at and reflect on their linguistic and cultural activities as well as critical incidents from their lived experiences. They also create uptake documents in which they discuss their choices and provide a rationale and reflection after critically analyzing their own productions, assumptions and understandings of various linguistic, cultural and societal ideologies shaping their ideas and actions on writing.

Keywords: translingualism, linguistic identity, language ideologies, language variation, correct English fallacy, language and power, linguistic narratives

***

Introduction

In light of the changing demographics and linguistic realities of educational contexts, it is no longer the case that students in US college composition classrooms are native-speakers of English, though most considered to be so by default (Matsuda). As a result, in the era of post-monolingualism (Yildiz), FYC programs are transnational spaces, and it is necessary to adapt to these changes. Therefore, in such diverse landscapes, how writing instructors respond to translingual and transnational needs and enact relevant pedagogies becomes highly important.

To this end, drawing from the growing body of research in translingualism (Motha, Jain, and Tecle; Canagarajah "Negotiating"; "Toward a Writing"; Ayash) and writing program ecologies (Reiff et al.), as a writing instructor in a predominantly white and monolingual midwestern university, I design and teach FYC courses around the themes of language and cultural diversity. In doing so, I use the frameworks embraced and utilized in our award-winning Writing Program built around rhetorical genre studies, cultural-historical activity theory, and translingualism. In that sense, both in the writing program and the English department, the whole ecology allows writing instructors to design courses around the nine learning outcomes, two of which specifically focus on cultural and linguistic diversity in writing.

In this chapter, I describe a unit plan on cultural and linguistic diversity in writing along with the materials I use and the writing prompts I provide students with to increase their awareness of linguistic diversity and how culture, along with other identity aspects and individual factors, influences one's literate activities. I end the unit with the project of linguistic and cultural trajectory narrative in which they look at and reflect on their linguistic and cultural activities as well as critical incidents from their lived experiences to revisit their understandings of how composition and writing takes place. They also create uptake documents in which they discuss their choices and provide a rationale and reflection after critically analyzing their own productions, assumptions, and understandings of various linguistic, cultural, and societal ideologies shaping their ideas and actions on writing.

Translingualism as Theorized

Translingualism and translingual literacy, both in applied linguistics and composition studies, have received great attention as a language ideology to address variation in language use and its implications on students' writing development as well as teaching of writing in the diverse era of language use (see Canagarajah *Literacy*; Jain; Horner et al.; Horner and Lu; Motha, Jain, and Tecle; Pennycook). Due to the changing demographics and linguistic realities in the world and in the US specifically, the need to move away from traditional approaches to teaching and viewing writing has led to linguistic ideologies like translingualism, which one can argue began with the impactful work of Horner et al. in 2011. Viewing language as fluid, mobile, and negotiable, translingualism has set out to eschew standard written English and unaccented speech concepts and unrealistic language uniformity. Additionally, it has added to our understanding that any language variety users have in their repertoire and use can indeed be seen and be taken advantage of as linguistic resources rather than deficiencies and hindrances to one's linguistic capabilities when introduced to a new literacy context. The divergences from the 'standard' or any variety not recognized or accepted by the English monolingualism ideology advocates have started to be seen as conscious moves by the language users. As Canagarajah ("The Place" 609) also puts it, "Not every instance of nonstandard usage by a student is an unwitting error; sometimes it is an active choice motivated by important cultural and ideological considerations" thus empowering the users by recognizing their agentic power. Seeing writers as not boxed in by narrow terms linguistically and/or culturally, but as reshaped as translingual writers who are engaged in movements across linguistic systems where genres, languages, disciplines, and different writing systems, with this relatively new ideology, negotiating language difference has become the key to understanding and appreciating linguistic diversity.

To this end, Canagarajah states that we should look at the understanding of production, circulation, and reception of texts that are always mobile, drawing from diverse languages, symbol systems, and modalities of communication, involving inter-community negotiations ("Negotiating"). However, as Ayash proposes, we are in an era called 'postmonolingualism', which is a 'surrogate' to monolingualism in that English monolingualism is still existent and in-effect. To this end, in order to facilitate these negotiations on language difference and variation, collaboration with scholars and practitioners across the subdisciplines of English is needed, because as Matsuda states, in an effort to fill the gap in the practical area in translingual research, though much has been done at the theoretical front, it has not been sufficient yet to create a turn in the field with sustainable movements and there is a need for interdisciplinarity because a lot that has been said and done in regards to translingualism in applied linguistics is being introduced to composition studies as new ideas ("The Myth"). Through collaboration across disciplines and scholars, then, by building on the theorizations so far put forth, the practical front can also gain more momentum. In that sense, what Matsuda suggests is that there is still much interdisciplinary work to do to get the full benefits that translingualism has to offer. This is part of my goal in this chapter, too, that by drawing from my scholarship and experience from applied linguistics and writing studies, I make use of a variety of materials in my FYC classes to help my students realize and appreciate their linguistic repertoires and translinguality to make better use of their resources moving forward.

University Context

The university in which I design and teach the FYC courses is a public university in the Midwest that emphasizes teaching and learning, offering degrees and programs at the bachelor, master, and doctoral levels. In Fall of 2018, out of 20,635 students enrolled, 18,107 were undergraduates, and ¼ of this population was from underrepresented backgrounds ("About"). From these undergraduate enrollments, the university factbook states 13,209 were White while 1,683 African American, 1,997 Hispanic, 576 had two or more responses (excluding Hispanic), 388 Asian, 164 Non-U.S. citizens, 19 American Indian or Alaskan Native, and 18 were Hawaiian or Pacific Islander (and 53 chose not to respond) ("Students-Total Enrollment" 21). From the freshman population of 4,808 students, 3,129 identified as White, and 96.3% of students from the U.S. were residents of Illinois. And although there is no data showing the linguistic background of these populations, International Statistics show that from the new enrollments in Fall of 2018, 145 were international students, mainly coming from India, Ghana, China, Bangladesh and South Korea ("International Statistics"). Although it is not clear how many of these international students are enrolled in FYC, from my own experience of teaching in the WP for more than six semesters, I can say it is usually only a handful across all sections.

As for the Writing Program (WP) situated in the English Department, recognized by CCCC Certificate of Excellence Award in 2014, rhetorical genre studies, cultural-historical activity theory, and translingualism are used as the foundational theories to frame the work we do.

With a history of more than 30 years, the WP offers more than 60 sections of ENG101 (Composition as Critical Inquiry), 10 sections of ENG101.10, and ENG145 and ENG145.13 (Writing in the Academic Disciplines and Writing Business and Government Organizations respectively). The most recent data (2014) shows that these courses are taught by 75 instructors, 62 of whom are graduate teaching instructors ("Program Explanations and Philosophies"). In the courses offered, the learning outcomes the conceptual frameworks provide are gathered around nine[1], and by taking each of these learning outcomes as a basis, we as instructors employ various activities and assignments along with class discussions, and we have the freedom to create course plans according to our scholarly interests and themes we are interested in as long as we address these learning outcomes. And although the required course text is the in-house *Grassroots Writing Research Journal* (GWRJ) and its previous issues, we can also make use of any outside texts to fit with our own goals and objectives.

Translingualism Enacted in ENG101: Composition as Critical Inquiry: Language and Identity

When I first designed my course as *Language and/as Identity*, I started my first class with a quote from Gloria Anzaldúa, "I am my language" (53), which ended up on my syllabus for the following semesters. I did this to inform my students that language is the core of who we are and what we do with it determines and showcases our linguistic identities. With that in mind, each semester, we start with the course rationale and discuss the themes of language and identity and how issues surrounding language, ways we negotiate our meanings in different forms of communication, and more importantly, *why* we feel the need to do so. To this end, by focusing on the individuality, agency, and creativity in language use, I intend to address how we can explore our writer-researcher identities by critically analyzing and reflecting on our own and others' linguistic choices to communicate content and meaning in the most efficient way to accomplish certain purposes with one's intended audience in a specific genre. Using this rhetorical approach to writing with an emphasis on critical genre analyses and consecutively production, I aim to increase student awareness of the power of language in analyzing and creating various compositions. In doing so, I draw from scholars in the field of applied linguistics and second language writing as well as composition studies, and taking Matsuda's suggestion on interdisciplinary collaboration, I aim to address especially the last two learning outcomes in our writing program:

LO 8: Cultures and Communities: Culturally responsive and ethical representations in writing

LO 9: Translingual and transnational literacies: Attention to diverse language practices

Though I address the other learning outcomes, both in this unit and the rest of the course, these two learning outcomes mainly constitute the unit details I share in this chapter. I have taught this unit on translingualism and transnationalism in writing and communication for three semesters as of Spring 2020, and though I make some changes in the way I teach these concepts each semester depending on student responses, I mainly make use of similar materials.

Genres and Language(s): Raising students' awareness in language variations

After establishing writing program concepts and detailing the frameworks we will be using during the semester, we start our discussions on translingualism right away. Since the term is relatively a new one and almost none of the students have heard it before, I ask them what they think the meaning of the prefix *trans-* brings to a word it attaches to by giving them a list of words with this prefix. They make guesses like 'change', 'transfer', or 'across' and by building on their guesses, we focus on the differences between concepts of monolingualism, bilingualism, and multilingualism as they frequently tend to associate the term with multilingualism. Though they are familiar with these terms in relation to the number of languages one knows, when it comes to distinguishing them from translingualism, they seem to have some struggles at first. However, I give them detailed explanations along with excerpts from scholars such as Canagarajah and Horner et al., as well as some texts from our GWRJ which address the topic. Although the excerpts and definitions I present seem too abstract for them initially, the readings from our textbook give them the basics to move further more smoothly.

After going over the theoretical aspects of translingualism, I have them do some individual exercises to help them realize that they, too, are translingual even though they may not realize it. One way I do this is to have them go online and take the *New York Times* Dialect Quiz ("How Y'all, Youse and You Guys Talk"), which has 25 questions on dialectical differences on daily language use, from pronunciation to lexical preferences for, for instance, soda-pop, y'all- youse- you guys and water fountain-bubbler, among others. The test then gives a visual map of where in the U.S. the users might likely be from based on their responses. The three regions they get based on their dialectical choices then create fruitful discussions in class. As a transnational person myself, I take the test again every time I ask my students to take it and share my results with them, which show a great deal of difference each time, and I make clear to my students the likely reasons for these differences. Their responses can also be unexpected sometimes; some get regions they have never even been before while some get a region only one of their relatives lives in. This creates great discussion opportunities and urges them to think more critically about the underlying reasons such as what they are exposed to growing up, the various interactions they have with various people, or what they read, watch, or consume in general. After demonstrating through this dialect test that even seemingly so similar group of people (students who are mostly from the Chicago area, in their late teens, who self-identify as monolingual English speakers) the variations they see among themselves set the tone for the rest of the unit as they become intrigued by the concept of translingualism and see that whatever knowledge and experiences they bring from their diverse background are great resources. We end that week by reading a GWRJ article titled 'Language variation across genres: Translingualism here and there' by Cristine Sánchez-Martín and students write in their journals a response to the prompt: 'In the article Cristina says: 'Translingualism helps us cross social barriers' (39). To cross this barrier, language plays a crucial role. How do you think a 'Non-Standard' approach to language help you achieve this?' With this reading and writing, I intend to have them think about the variations in writing and not just spoken language and how monolingual ideologies can create discrimination and social issues.

The next class starts with a focus on differences in writing in the same genres across languages and cultures as a follow-up to the last reading we do. Students get into groups and are asked to gather three samples of the genres they are given: wedding invitations, CVs, and recipes, from different languages and cultures. Once they collect their samples, they compare them to what they know of these genres and analyze them critically through a set of questions that Cultural-Historical Activity Theory provides us with. They create a list of the conventions they know of these genres to have and then create another list with their observations of the samples from other languages and cultures. They identify the similarities and differences among them and share what they find with the class. Once the common conventions are established, students are asked to create a sample of the genre they are given (making changes as they want) to represent the variety of English (or other languages they know/use) and provide the rest of the class with necessary explanations of why they did what they did. This rationale for their choices, explaining why they kept certain conventions while changing some, for instance, gives them the opportunity to negotiate their content and meaning when they present their productions to the class. At the end of the class, they are also asked to write their daily entries focusing their reflections on the way language is used in the written form within those genres across languages and cultures and what they have learned about different usages of language from their peers' research and presentations. Depending on how we structure these, it may take more than one class period to get to all of the presentations. And depending on the interests of the instructors or the students, the genres chosen for this could also be Wikipedia pages, music videos, or driver's license to show the different values given in constructing, delivering and communicating knowledge. So, whatever they analyze as part of the activity (invitations, CV, music video etc.), they also create one based on their own goals and rationale for the choices they make in producing their own versions of the genre.

Correct English Fallacy: Challenging Standard English

In another class, we watch a TED Talk by Kellam Barta in which he brings out issues like AAE, vocal fry, or generational differences in language use ("No such thing as correct English"), in continuation of variations in composition and writing across languages and cultures and in an effort to bring in relatable materials. We pull out some sentences that stand out such as correct and acceptable definitions of privilege and seeing language variation as difference and celebration rather than deficiency or laziness or random choices, which correlate really well with translingualism, which and then connects to concepts of monolingual ideology and linguistic imperialism. After discussing the dangers of such discriminatory approaches to language difference, especially when it targets certain groups of people and becomes an identity issue, we turn our attention again to translingualism and what it has to offer as disposition to openness and inquiry. This video also reminds them of the dialect quiz we have taken earlier in the unit and how they negotiated their own differences with the rest of the class by presenting on the possible defensible reasons for such variations.

After discussing the concept of "correct English" fallacy through this video, I then introduce them to Robert Kaplan's Contrastive Rhetoric and show them his doodles to talk about organizational and rhetorical patterns differing among languages and how a person's first language and other linguistic repertoires can influence how they write in another language or register or code. Since English is represented through a direct line, they can immediately say that they write straightforward and simple in English, but seeing the organizational patterns of other languages in Kaplan's doodles, they are intrigued as to how other people use language to communicate, not just in written language but also spoken. Some also identify their way of telling a story and how they organize their information in a given text with the other doodles given such as 'oriental' or 'romance'. Then, I have them watch at least the first part of the three-part documentary *Writing Across Borders* written and directed by Wayne Robertson (2010) where they see some people with differing linguistic backgrounds discussing how to tell a story: leaving the main point to the end or using a lot of details as opposed to English where their own experiences have mostly been with writing thesis and topic sentences at the very beginning, for instance. For many of them, 'the English way' has been the only way to write an essay, so they usually find it really interesting to see how people form arguments in writings in other languages. They sometimes ask me questions about composing in Turkish, and they like hearing about my experiences with writing within and across languages. I have not done this myself yet but am planning to next semester: at this point, we can ask students to interview someone (a friend, professor, or even a family member) for whom English is not the first language or they have learned writing in another language, preferably through schooling, to share their responses with the class later on. Such an assignment can lead to discussions on why English has such power, especially in academic settings, and the implications for this power on the other languages and dialects. If students have not even taken any foreign language courses before, this insight into the experiences of other linguistically resourceful people can help them gain more awareness in variations of language use.

Varieties of English: Myth of linguistic homogeneity

In the next class, we watch another TED Talk titled "Why I keep speaking up even when people mock my accent" by Safwat Saleem. As we watch, we take notes on what stands out to us. After talking about our notes, I make sure we also touch upon what it means to be labeled 'normal' or 'abnormal' and thus become 'invisible', the societal expectations of being too self-conscious and overcorrecting our language or behaviors, discriminations faced based on favoritism, and ways to challenge the narrow definitions of normalism and what is at stake if we do not. With this video, I urge them to think beyond the accented speech that causes discrimination but and more towards other sorts of discriminations faced, as well. We may share the discriminations we have faced and how we responded to them as well as what we can do moving forward. As we move further into the class, I bring in the concept of World Englishes and Three Circle Model of Kachru to show them how prevalent the power of English is and how it functions in different contexts. To move away from the theoretical part of the plurality of Englishes, I then show them translingual signs around the world, some have been collected by myself and some available online or from scholarly resources, which include creative expressions in Chinglish, Spanglish, or Turklish. What I try to emphasize here is how people respond to certain needs through their language and how what might seem 'abnormal' to their English actually works perfectly in other contexts, and that language is fluid and happens in negotiation among the members of its users. Then, I ask them to find and bring their own examples of such usages and discuss where they might be being used or for what purposes, what they think they might mean or why they are used in those 'non-standard' ways. Seeing that, especially in metropolitan areas, how there are indeed translingual and transnational communities, such as in China towns, for instance, the students tend to become more aware of their surroundings and the diversity that they already live with and in, and that come to see linguistic homogeneity as something that does not actually exist.

Challenging single stories: The power of language

In the following classes where we focus more on diversity and how language affects perceptions and that words matter, I start by asking students the meaning/definition of the word 'alien', and after a few minutes, I show them Google images showing extraterrestrial creatures appearing with the word alien. I then show them signs from airports and 'resident alien' ID cards for foreigners living in the US and ask them who might be deciding on the use of 'alien' in such a context and why they might have chosen it and the implications of calling a human being 'alien'. I am aware (and make it known to the students, as well) that the primary meaning of the word is 'a person of another family, race or nation' ("Alien") but I also want to point out the prevalent usage in daily language and how it can create undesired effects. Our discussion continues with a focus on power relations, then, the danger of labels and assigned identities in different communities, all paving the way for Adichie's TED Talk on "The danger of a single story". We watch it carefully and we discuss important concepts that appear in the video such as stereotypes, one representing all, being abject, prejudices we face, immigration, misconceptions, descriptions such as half-devil half-child, among many others and their implications for the receiver of such notions. After the discussion, I give students three prompts to write about for the day, and they can choose one or more to respond to: (1) How does being exposed to the different versions of the same story affect our assumptions/ knowledge building?, (2) How do you think our 'assigned' identities affect the way we speak/behave/live/write?, and (3) What do you understand from 'gaining paradise' through writing?

Our discussions on assigned identities and social labels continue with two short online articles, which students read in two groups. The articles are titled "How labels like black and working class shape identity" (Alter) and "On the power of words, labels, and language: do no harm" (Heffernan). When they are done reading, each student reading one of the articles is matched with another one reading the other one, and they retell the gist of the articles to each other. Some students summarize the articles and what they take away from them and how they connect to the larger theme of the class and the unit. We end the class by reflecting on some concepts taken from the readings such as being 'willing to view the world with the guidance of labels when faced with an otherwise unbreakable tie', the power of expectations and self-fulfilling prophecies, and use of labels about mental illness, disability, and economic status. With these materials and critical discussions, I aim to have them think about the power of language and the implications of (language) ideologies as well as stereotyping and the ethical considerations of all these on individuals as well as society.

To go further into addressing issues related to culture and communication and to emphasize that culture, however narrow or broad we define it, is not the sole factor influencing how we communicate. I remind them of the concept of contrastive rhetoric, but this time, I bring in Intercultural Rhetoric (Connor et al.) asking them what the differences might be or why one might prefer one over the other. Talking about the advantages and disadvantages of these lenses in thinking about the relationship between language and culture as well as individual factors that directly influence one's writing, we then point out how easily we can engage in cultural essentialism. To emphasize the individual factors that influence our linguistic identities, or how we communicate in the world, we also take an online personality test ("16personalities") and read about our traits, strengths and weaknesses. After giving them enough time to explore their traits in relation to academics, relationships, or career (to name a few), I urge them to think about how these traits might relate to how they compose and write in certain genres and under certain circumstances of communication across different discourses. Taking into account various people they interact with, various genres they consume and produce, and various physical and geographical realities they find themselves in, I ask them to create a linguistic map and present it in class. They can draw, make a collage, or create videos if they want to best represent their linguistic identities. With this, they can see even a simple reading activity for a class can be accomplished in so many different ways by different people. Depending on time, we watch another TED talk given by a cognitive scientist on how languages shape the way we think (Boroditsky) to have them think more on the individual factors influencing our communication. The presenter who talks about how the human mind is influenced by the language we speak, by giving examples from different speech communities as to giving directions, describing colors, grammatical gender, or event descriptions using active/passive structures. I end the class by giving them a prompt from the video: 'Boroditsky says that human minds have invented not one cognitive universe, but 7,000. How does your universe is shaped by your language or how does it shape your language? Pick a quote or two from the video and explain your linguistic identity and universe.'

End of unit assignment: Linguistic and cultural trajectory narrative

With that last bit of writing on cognitive universes, we can move on to the end-of-unit assignment on linguistic and cultural trajectory narrative, for which they can draw from their in-class writings as well as classroom discussion notes or any material we have covered throughout the unit. Before they draft their own narratives, though, I have them read my own. I give this narrative assignment because I believe it gives ample opportunities for students to not only discover their language and culture, but it also gives *me* a sense of their responses to the unit. On such assignments, Cavazos (49) says: "Literacy histories or narratives are common assignments in fyw courses, and as Christina Ortmeier-Hooper suggests, they are an excellent tool for instructors to learn about their students' experiences (414-15)." In addition to the benefit of learning about students' experiences, this linguistic and cultural narrative also gives students the advantage of digging deeper into their own experiences and revisit them with fresh and new perspectives they have hopefully gained in the unit. Using their antecedent knowledge and experiences with language use, they can have a more critical approach to their own beliefs, values, and understandings and these approaches can help them move forward in more confidence in their abilities surrounding writing and composition as it is an empowering process to value one's own resources. Many of my students who did the assignment in the previous semesters stated that they appreciated it because of how personal it was which was unprecedented to them. They also repeatedly mentioned that they started to see themselves as valuable resources in academic contexts. This critical awareness of one's own knowledge and experiences in turn increases student engagement and motivation, and students are more willing to take risks in their writing.

While we go over once more the guidelines for the project, I also ask them to respond to the sample narrative I have written. Sometimes I also bring in examples from student work from previous semesters if I have their permission, but the reason I choose to include my own writing sample is firstly because I want them to see that whatever I ask them to do, I try it myself and then explain to them what the process has been like for me. That way, I can also partly experience the struggles they might face and try to anticipate them in advance and share with them how I have responded to them. Also, this gives them an opportunity to get to know me as an instructor better because my transnational identity seems interesting to them for the most part and they might be hesitant to ask direct questions. My personal lived experiences with translingual and transnational writing shape how I conduct myself in different activity systems as well as through different social roles I take. I begin with how I learned English in a foreign language context but in an English-medium American-origin university strictly following 'standard' English forms without paying attention to the local realities, how I moved to Spain to teach English in a school where British English was prioritized and valued and students' linguistic resources were mostly ignored, and then experiencing the same back in my country, Turkey, at college level, as an instructor employing and enforcing 'standard' English and ignoring local realities which at some point made me pause and re-assess my whole identity as a life-long language learner and English teacher. I share that this final experience made me find my way back to the academia to explore the intricacies of shuttling between languages and varieties in different contexts, cultures, and communities. These details from my narrative help them structure their own while providing them some ideas for content. However, I make sure to emphasize over and over again that what matters the most with all these major assignments are the uptake documents that accompany them. In their uptake documents, they not only give their rationale for their genre and content choices to deliver what they value in relation to who they are and what their languages are like, but they also critically reflect on their processes with a specific focus on the realizations, where their antecedent knowledge and experiences are disrupted, and how their thinking about a specific concept has changed. In these uptake documents, they are to describe explicitly how they incorporate new knowledge into their existing knowledge-thinking about who they were, are, and will likely be, and how their thinking about a specific situation has transformed with the new input/experience. In short, they are to *show* their learning throughout the unit. After some class time spent on drafting and revising, we do peer reviews and give each other feedback – based on guidelines (see Appendix) on the parts they think are necessary before submitting the final drafts for grading.

Conclusion

The university context and the majority of the student and faculty population being not very diverse, my main goal in creating a unit based on translingualism and transnationality is to increase student awareness on how these concepts are enacted in different ways of composing and the underlying factors and limiting language ideologies behind certain choices made in the process of production, delivery and reception of these compositions. To this end, my making use of resources available in the immediate ecology of WP and the English department allow ample space for us instructors to design and teach FYC as freely as possible around the learning outcomes that pay specific focus on diverse ways of communication and language use. Without the support of faculty and administration and explicit attention to culture, communities and translingual and transnational literacies, I suspect, we would have many struggles to bring these concerns to the surface in our classrooms. Using our diverse scholarly interests and experiences as resources adds to the benefits of embracing such interdisciplinary pedagogies. Seeing that students also value such insights and discussions on such important and immediate social issues in class, I continue to bring these to the forefront every time I design and revisit my course plans.

Works Cited

"16personalities." NERIS Analytics Limited. https://www.16personalities.com/. Accessed December 14, 2020.

"About." Illinois State University, https://illinoisstate.edu/about/. Accessed January 15, 2020.

Adichie, Chimamanda. "The Danger Of A Single Story." *Youtube*, uploaded by TED, October 7, 2009, https://www.youtube.com/watch?v=D9Ihs241zeg

"Alien." Merriam-Webster, https://www.merriam-webster.com/dictionary/alien, 2020.

Alter, Adam. "How labels like black and working class shape identity." *The Week*. May 4, 2013. https://theweek.com/articles/464854/how-labels-like-black-working-class-shape-identity. Accessed December 12, 2020.

Anzaldúa, Gloria E. *Borderlands*. San Francisco, USA: Aunt Lute Books, 1987.

Ayash, Nancy Bou. *Toward Translingual Realities in Composition: (Re)Working Local Language Representations and Practices*, Louisville, Utah State University Press, 2019.

Barta, Kellam. "No such thing as correct English." *Youtube*, uploaded by TEDx Talks, August 30, 2016. Youtube video. https://www.youtube.com/watch?v=VEFM905EOUk

Boroditsky, Lera. "How Languages Shape The Way We Think." *Youtube*, uploaded by TED, May 2, 2018. Youtube video. https://www.youtube.com/watch?v=RKK7wGAYP6k&t=382s

Canagarajah, Athelstan Suresh. "Toward a Writing Pedagogy of Shuttling Between Languages: Learning from Multilingual Writers." *College English*, vol 68, no 6, 2006, pp 589-604.

—. "The Place Of World Englishes In Composition: Pluralization Continued." *College Composition and Communication*, vol 57, no. 4, 2006, pp 586-619.

—. "Negotiating Translingual Literacy: An Enactment." *Research in the Teaching of English* vol 48, no. 1, 2013, pp 40-67.

—. Editor. *Literacy As Translingual Practice: Between Communities And Classrooms*. New York: Routledge, 2013.

Cavazos, Alyssa. G. "Encouraging languages other than English in First-Year Writing Courses: Experiences from linguistically diverse writers." *Composition Studies*, vol 47, no 1, 2019, pp 38-56.

Connor, Ulla, et al., editors, *Contrastive Rhetoric Reaching to Intercultural Rhetoric*. John Benjamins Publishing, 2008.

Heffernan, Pat. "On the power of words, labels, and language: do no harm." *Change Conversations*, March 8, 2018. https://www.marketing-partners.com/conversations2/on-the-power-of-words-labels-and-language-do-no-harm. Accessed December 12, 2020.

Horner, Bruce., et al. "Toward A Multilingual Composition Scholarship: From English Only To A Translingual Norm." *College Composition and Communication*, vol 63, no. 2, 2011, pp 269-300.

Horner, Bruce., et al. (2011). "Language Difference In Writing: Toward A Translingual Approach." *College English*, vol 73, no. 3, 2011, pp 303-321.

Horner, Bruce., and Min-Zhan Lu. "Translingual Literacy, Language Difference, and Matters of Agency." *College English*, vol 75, no. 6, 2013, pp 582-607.

"How Y'all, Youse and You Guys Talk." By Josh Katz and Wilson Andrews. The New York Times, December 21st, 2013. https://www.nytimes.com/interactive/2014/upshot/dialect-quiz-map.html, Accessed December 10, 2020.

"International Statistics: Fall 2018 Student Statistics". Office of International Studies and Programs. https://internationalstudies.illinoisstate.edu/students-scholars/about-isss/statistics/ Accessed Jan 15, 2020.

Jain, Rashi. "Global Englishes, Translinguistic Identities, and Translingual Practices in a Community College ESL Classroom: A Practitioner Research Reports." *TESOL Journal*, vol 5, no. 3, 2014, pp 490-518.

Kachru, Braj B. "Standards, Codification, And Sociolinguistic Realism: The English Language In The Outer Circle." In *English in the World: Teaching And Learning The Language And The Literature*, edited by Randolph Quirk and Henry Widdowson, 1985, Cambridge: Cambridge University Press.

Kaplan, Robert B. "Cultural Thought Patterns in Inter-Cultural Education." *Language Learning*, vol 16, no. 1-2, 1966, pp 1-20.

Matsuda, Paul Kei. "The Myth Of Linguistic Homogeneity In U.S. College Composition." *College English*, vol 68, no. 6, 2006, pp 637-651.

—. "It's the Wild West Out There: A New Linguistic Frontier in U.S. College Composition" *Literacy As Translingual Practice: Between Communities And Classrooms*, edited by Suresh Canagarajah, 2013, pp 128-138.

Motha, Suhanthie., et al. "Translinguistic Identity-as-Pedagogy: Implications for Language Teacher Education." *International Journal of Innovation in English Language Teaching*, vol 1, no. 1, 2012, pp 13-28.

Ortmeier-Hooper, Christina. "'English May Be My Second Language, but I'm not ESL.'" College Composition and Communication, vol. 59, no. 3, 2008, 389-419.

Pennycook, Alastair. "Language Education as Translingual Activism." *Asia Pacific Journal of Education*, vol 26, no. 1, 2006, pp 111-114.

—. *Global Englishes and Transcultural Flows*. New York, Routledge, 2007.

—. "English As A Language Always In Translation." *European Journal of English Studies* vol 12, no. 1, 2008, pp 33-47.

"Program Explanations and Philosophies". Grassroots Writing Research: Illinois State University.http://isuwriting.com/program-explanation-and-philosophies/. Accessed January 15, 2020.

Reiff, Mary J, et al., editors. *Ecologies of Writing Programs: Program Profiles in Context.* Anderson: Parlor Press, 2015.

Saleem, Safwat. "Why I keep speaking up even when people mock my accent". *Youtube,* uploaded by TED, August 15, 2016, https://www.youtube.com/watch?v=B4a0NvLTebw

Sánchez-Martín, Cristina. "Language Variation Across Genres: Translingualism Here And There." *Grassroots Writing Research Journal,* vol 7, no. 1, 2016, pp 33-43.

"Students-Total Enrollment". University Factbook, https://prpa.illinoisstate.edu/downloads/Fall%202018%20Factbook%20Final%20-%20Updated%20S2F%20Ratio.pdf, Accessed January 15, 2020.

Writing Across Borders. Directed by Wayne Robertson. Oregon State University: Center for Writing and Learning and Writing Intensive Curriculum Program, *Youtube,* uploaded by Nachtjagdgeschwader, May 15, 2010, https://www.youtube.com/watch?v=quI0vq9VF-c

Yildiz, Yasemin. *Beyond the Mother Tongue: The Postmonolingual Condition,* New York, Fordham University Press, 2012.

Appendix A

Linguistic and Cultural Trajectory Narrative: Unit Project Guidelines

In short, you will compose your own linguistic and cultural trajectory narratives, thinking about your past experiences with language use and learning, taking into consideration the different discourses- people with whom you interact(ed), the social aspects of the situations, the power relations at play which influence your choices and reflect how all these factors have an effect in the way you (re)construct your *selves* as writer-researchers by supporting your arguments with the relevant class materials.

Stories we tell make us who we are and shape how we view and interact with the world. Reflections that we make as we compose stories about ourselves are necessary to develop a cultural and linguistic competence in our interactions as individuals. Therefore, this project is designed to help raise awareness on the different ways our identities (our language, race, gender, class, sexual orientation or ethnicity etc) influence our actions, and overall perspectives about the world. The purpose is to give you an opportunity to express your linguistic and cultural identity in a way that is appealing to you. Specifically, this project asks you to share an autobiographical/auto-ethnographic story of how your experiences with languages and cultures impact who you are today.

We have seen various videos or read some articles where people from diverse backgrounds share their stories and we discussed how what they have experienced shape who they are as writers/researchers/composers. Similarly, your story should also include:

- Specific examples that have had an important impact on your thinking about language, culture, ethical considerations, etc.

- How your experiences or your specific background have shaped how you view composition and how you see yourself as a writer-researcher

- Any people who have been influential in your trajectory/your identity journey- which is also reflected in the way you communicate with the world

Some of the guiding questions include but are not limited to the following: How would you define your languages/language variations and cultures? If you don't speak or write in a second language, what have been your experiences like with languages (and speakers of those languages) other than your own? What cultural and linguistic experiences make you who you are? What are some of the critical events, cultural practices or people that had an impact on your writer-researcher identity today? Why does this critical incident/event matter to you? What linguistic or cultural stereotypes existed when you were growing up? How do you think such stereotypes affect the way you view linguistic diversity today? What are some of the cultural and linguistic values and beliefs you bring with you to your academic discourse?

While the genre and delivery/ design of this project may vary, it is important that you create a flowing narrative that gives the reader a sense of your evolving identity as a writer-researcher who deeply cares about issues revolving around linguistic diversity in a wide range of contexts. Make sure to choose a genre that would represent all these in the best/ most efficient way, and at the end of your project include your rationale for choosing the genre you have for this particular purpose. You may choose to write an autobiographical narrative in the form of poems, make a video accompanied with photos and a narrative, provide interviews, personal accounts and anecdotes, or experiment with other kinds of multimodal writing. In short, Feel free to be creative and incorporate multiple forms of expression into your writing (e.g. drawing, photos, poems, cartoons, children's book, podcast etc) if you think that best represents who you are and best fits with your genre expectations and audience and your goals with the project.

Uptake document for the project

In your uptake document, please discuss the following points in as much detail as possible:

- Why you chose the genre for your delivery- what it communicates about you and your writerly identity,

- Reasoning of your choices in structuring/organizing your piece (subsections, specific examples and specific course materials included)

- What else you would have liked to include and why

- Strengths and weaknesses of your piece

- Any struggles of problems encountered and how you have overcome them

Your take-away points for this project: What is the most important thing you learned with this project and how do you think it affects who you are as a writer?

Part 3.
Creating Temporary Transnational Space through Assignment Design

The section following includes two chapters in which the authors offer unique assignment designs to achieve their distinct but related student learning outcomes. The authors in this section have either created one-off assignments that create temporary transnational spaces or use reflections from instructors to evaluate the effectiveness of transnational assignments. While the previous sections evaluated the efficacy of a transnational themed course, these authors are attempting to add specific assignments that would augment with their current course objectives. The research in these chapters is motivated to refine a transnational assignment as a way of satisfying a market demand for transnational competency.

In Maria Houston and Ekaterina Gradaleva's chapter, *Learning by Writing: Possibilities of Tele-Collaborative Transnational Education In and Beyond an FYW Classroom*, the authors explore the efficacy of a transnational assignment that uses digital platforms to facilitate collaborative learning. They synthesize theoretical works from Carnagarajah and Pennycook as well as work on digital literacy from Robert Shutter with data collected by Starosta and Olorunnisola in 1998 and McEwan and Sobre-Denton in 2011 on the affective aspects of writing. The chapter provides curriculum and assignment that have the specific purpose of equipping students with marketable writing skills they can use to list on their resumes. The assignment created, the *International Conference Project*, is meant to equip students with transnational/transcultural composition skills that can improve their aptitude in transnational workplaces. Evidence they gather suggests there are economic as well as ethical reasons why transnational pedagogy should be incorporated in the classroom. Houston and Gradaleva justify their methods by referring to digital literacy requirements in the current job market. The need for students to obtain high levels of electracy can be addressed by the same assignment used to create a transnational space - specifically to students in a rural/suburban town. Their work is uniquely valuable to transnational pedagogy because of its capital-centered perspective.

The chapter following takes an alternative approach to assignment design research. Authors Phuong Minh Tran, Kyle J. Lucas, and Kenneth Tanemura are graduate students whose research consists of analyzing over a dozen transnational assignments to demonstrate ways transnational spaces can and should be a part of the learning outcomes for first-year writing students. Like Houston and Gradaleva, they claim the increased transnationalism in higher education demand instructors incorporate some sort of translingual writing assignment. This chapter offers literary synthesis followed by comprehensive secondary research that highlights the common objectives teachers of transnationalism have sought to accomplish and assignments teachers have used to accomplish their goals. Through a lucid structure, the authors build on ideas from Carnagarajah, Horner, Martin, Guerra, and Tardy to synthesize and draw a comparative analysis on previously applied translingual pedagogies in transnational spaces in order to deduce common achievements and shortcomings of transnational student learning outcomes. By comparing the data from these assignments, the authors help teachers assess which types of assignments might help them achieve their transnational learning outcomes.

These chapters depict the results of translingual assignments implemented to create transnational environments. This section is valuable for teachers who would like to incorporate small changes to their current courses rather than build a curriculum or design a course from scratch.

Chapter 7

Learning by Writing: Possibilities of Tele-Collaborative Transnational Education In and Beyond a First-Year Writing Classroom

Maria Houston

Texas A&M University Texarkana

Ekaterina Gradaleva

Samara State Technical University

Abstract: While multilingual transnationals are widely represented in FYW classrooms across the nation, pedagogical and programming initiatives that foster the development of various linguistic, rhetorical, and cultural competences among freshmen writers who daily write and communicate with peers, professors, colleagues, neighbors, family and friends of multiple linguistic and national backgrounds fall behind. This chapter discusses a transnational, tele-collaborative, experiential learning project in which FYW students in the U.S. and second-year engineering majors in an English class in Russia worked in small transnational groups via interactive social media on identifying, researching, and presenting on globally meaningful topics. The chapter briefly describes the project and discusses at-length multiple positive learning outcomes as well as pedagogical and administrative challenges involved at various stages of its implementation. The authors conclude with a call for professional development for faculty willing to embrace a "transnational composition classroom" as well as concrete advice on managing such projects and learning in the classroom.

Keywords: transnational composition, transnational communicative competences, FYW programmatic innovations, tele-collaborative initiatives, transnational writing pedagogies, Interactive New Media, global writing initiatives

***

Education should be practical. Its effects should stretch beyond the academy. Its outcomes should provide access, mobility, and opportunity. Further, in a world so closely connected, no excuses exist for academics to not "carve" spaces for their students to engage in transnational negotiations and focus pedagogical efforts on the achievement of a constructive dialogue against all stereotypes and tangible and intangible borders. Aligned with the pivotal goals of education as outlined by the Council of Writing Program Administrators in a report titled "The Framework for Success in Postsecondary Writing," those were our thoughts when we started the process of designing the International Conference Project- a class-to-class transnational, virtual (developed, facilitated, and assessed via New Media) collaborative initiative between freshmen in a U.S. composition class and sophomores in an English class in Russia (Council of Writing Program Administrators 1). Our definition of "transnational" stems from the work by applied linguists (especially, Canagarajah's *Translingual Practice 31*) and incorporates any educational initiatives, pedagogical practices, processes, communicative encounters, etc. that involve parties from across the globe, are inherently collaborative, and engage multiple and varied communicative resources and repertoires brought into communication. Globalization, the World Wide Web, and increasing mobility shape a transnational communicative reality which transcends autonomous languages, cultures, and rhetorics with semiotic resources and modalities being indispensable participants of communication. Such a reality encouraged us to develop the ICP and explore the possibilities and affordances that this project brings to complement the transnational reality of our day and age.

Introduction by Maria Houston

As a composition instructor who, over the period of seven years, has taught at four universities across three states, I have come to observe a few similarities among freshmen in my first-year writing classrooms. First, they do not place much faith in a writing class that seems for them to hold no value beyond college walls. Second, an overwhelming majority of freshmen in my classes, at least, are convinced that they do not write outside of college and will not write anything close to the kind of writing they produce in college in the future. Finally, as I rediscover every first class of the semester, college freshmen overwhelmingly do not imagine that written communication coupled with "electracy" or facility with digital technologies are the most desired of college graduates' competencies on the job market today. Current socio-political and economic developments in the States and beyond continue to drive the demand for the above competencies. However, the Job Outlook Surveys by the

National Association of Colleges and Employers demonstrate year after year that U.S. graduates do not meet employer expectations ("Job Outlook Survey").

In the US only 35% of degrees are currently awarded to "white domestic students" (monolingual), while the rest go to multilinguals and multinationals (AAC&U). Cultural and linguistic diversity of college graduates mirror the environment in their prospective workplaces: In the 40 years between 1980 and 2020, the white working-age population in the United States declined from 83% of the nation's total to 63% while the number of minority workers has doubled. It has become common knowledge that millennials are the most diverse generation in the United States by self-identification and value system (Frey). Researchers predict a sharp increase in diverse multicultural and multilingual workplaces and teams where the biggest challenges would be overcoming conflict and fostering collaboration. The National Association of Colleges and Employers (NACE) identified teamwork/collaboration (ranks 3/10) and global/intercultural fluency (8/10) as key for career readiness today. In addition to stable growth of national diversity in the workplace, it is hard nowadays to come across a Fortune 100 that has not established some international presence (foreign sales, employees, partners, clients in a foreign country, etc.). Interestingly, many U.S.-based multinational companies make two-thirds of their profit overseas and have close to half or more foreign workers (Perry). Virtual written communication (emails, media reports, fact sheets, etc.) in such companies takes up a large portion of an everyday routine. Furthermore, the global enterprise collaboration market size is projected to grow through 2024 with the increasing use of networking websites and mobile devices for collaboration ("Global Enterprise Forecast"). This trend will continue to urge college writing curricula to catch up. I strongly believe that we absolutely must routinely demonstrate to our students that a) college writing empowers for a career, b) workplace writing with digital technologies is a real, everyday challenge, at modern workplaces, c) multiculturalism and multilingualism are the reality of professional communications in the increasingly global world. These trends in global professional communications, country demographics, and global economy prompted my colleague in Russia and I to take advantage of a feasible method, a Collaborative Research Project, and accessible-to-all New Media (Internet-based technology) to "carve" a hands-on, messy space for our students in two different countries to negotiate, make mistakes, and, through practice and guidance, gain confidence as communicators and "writers in the world" (Boyle).

Introduction by Ekaterina Gradaleva

I work at the Department of Linguistics, Cross-Cultural Communication, and Russian as a Foreign Language at Samara State Technical University and teach courses in English, Business English, and other courses related to cultural studies. Global enterprise drives transculturalism and virtual teams, where the ability to constructively negotiate across languages, rhetorics, and national values is crucial. When I was looking into a possibility of participating in a transnational writing and research project with a writing program within the U.S., I pursued interests and pedagogical insights in the transcultural domain. English instruction in Russia stretches beyond linguistic competency targeting the development of socio-cultural competency (also referred to as intercultural, transcultural, performative, etc.) which is defined as the formation of readiness and ability to sustain the dialogue of cultures (Solovova). Educators in the fields of Cultural Studies and Second Language Acquisition consider socio-cultural competency key for the success of transnational encounters (Byram, Solovova, Canagarajah, Karnyashev.) Such competency, while defined differently across fields and scholars, is generally viewed as a set of repertoires, resources (primarily, knowledge), and behaviors that subjects bring and utilize at the time of a transnational encounter. As Paran and Sercu pose, "school learning without direct contact with other cultures cannot lead to the development of intercultural competency" (31). While we study customs, traditions, communicative patterns, etc. of the U.S. in class and simulate transnational encounters in small-group dialogues and similar assignments, such practice is artificial and leaves little room for communicative mistakes and, as a result, for the creation of new communicative practices that are more successful. While the International Conference Project for my students and I was a unique chance to engage in real-life interactions with U.S. speakers of English who were "making mistakes", and work towards socio-cultural competency, it was also a way to transform the ecology of the space and place of the project into a true "third culture" where writing and language are not just signifying but also affective properties (Starosta and Olorunnisola; McEwan and Sobre-Denton). The idea is that when exchanging thoughts, ideas, and artifacts via interactive New Media, students in both countries will recognize that the purpose of such exchange is beyond mere information transfer towards the creation and transformation of participants into more aware, more confident, more productive researchers, scholars, and citizens. Finally, I wanted to explore the "real" dimensions and trajectories of socio-cultural competency especially as mediated by New Media and, as a result, create a more effective program for my course.

Towards a Vision of a Tele-Collaborative Transnational Writing Pedagogy

Transnational faculty-led initiatives, as we found, are unique in many ways. Ekaterina and I at the start of the project were situated, theoretically and pedagogically, in different fields and disciples. Each had her own unique goals and aspirations for the project. At the same time, we were both driven by similar desires: to provide our students with access to "real" communication in the world and, with our guidance, to develop their "archives" of repertoires and knowledge to succeed. Our differences worked to our benefit. For the sake of the Intercultural Conference Project, we needed to look at virtual transnational communication at an interdisciplinary level to absorb all/most existing knowledge for the success of the project. As post-humanistic orientation to writing and rhetoric gains ground, such disciplines as Cultural Studies, Applied Linguistics, Sociolinguistics are working full speed at developing praxis to close the gap between what we teach in school and what really happens in the world today. Intercultural New Media Studies (Shutter) offers valuable insights into various models of institutionalized new media intercultural encounters and practices as well as analytical frameworks to tackle such encounters; Applied Linguistics (Pennycook, Canagarajah) releases research that relates recent thinking about language use to concepts of space and conceptualizes languaging as inseparable from material resources and objects that create their own space or enters the subject's repertoire (Pennycook). Regardless of preparation, confidence, and control we perceived we had at the stage of implementation, the International Conference Initiative unfolded as a true post-humanistic ecological practice- a living body of its own. By undertaking this initiative, we both stepped into this living ecology of the International Conference Project and have received a continuous practice of "tuning up" and being "tuned up" by the elements within it and only the end goal stayed intact. Our hopes were that as a result of composing collaboratively across languages and borders in professional settings via the space of New Media our students will a) acknowledge and appreciate the complexity of real-life professional global communicative ecologies) develop various new "spatial répertoires", practices, and competencies to effectively communicate across languages, borders, and media (Pennycook).

Borrowing from post-humanistic praxis in Second Language and Intercultural Studies, we adopted a well-established format of "telecollaborative" classroom-to-classroom international exchange initiative to enact a post-humanistic orientation to language and rhetoric at a classroom level through engaging our students and ourselves in serial New Media encounters to help the students achieve their college objectives: competencies in alignment with the challenges of the current professional networked communicative landscape, employability, success.

In the following sections of the chapter we will:

a) Discuss the International Conference Project (ICP), its stages, goals, and elements with a focus on post-humanistic considerations in its design.

b) Reflect on the ICP as a "writing makes practice" initiative focusing on pedagogical, instructional, and administrative implications of networked collaborative transnational initiatives at a college level.

c) Consider the process and outcomes of the ICP, re-define socio-cultural competency and formulate the goals of networked transnational collaborative initiatives aimed at its development.

d) Discuss the role and the place of non-human in the networked communicative landscape of the global world with considerations to English Education and the global collaborative educational initiatives.

The International Conference Project: Stages, Elements, and Goals

In the spring of 2017, Ekaterina and I, driven by above aspirations and agendas, collaborated to design, implement, conduct, and evaluate a class-to-class partnership project: the International Youth Conference on Global Matters (ICP). The ICP engaged sophomores in an English as a Foreign Language class at a Technical College in Russia and freshmen at an Advanced Composition class at a private Catholic college in Ohio in a series of inquiry-based professional writing collaborative projects remotely presented at a Conference on Global Matters in Russia. The goal of the ICP was to allow students to analyze and evaluate their current composing practices in new media spaces and develop skills and competencies to "write in the world" for global audiences. In addition, the project would help all involved explore students' communicative practices across borders, modes, and media and devise new teaching methods, activities, and pedagogies to help students define and gain success in such communicative encounters in both personal and professional settings.

Post-humanism regards writing as an embodied interaction with other beings and the environment (Cooper 18). The International Conference project (ICP) was designed, implemented, and assessed remotely by means of Facebook (a public Facebook group and chats), Skype, and SurveyMonkey. Since we started planning the project, writing proposals, gaining administrative approval, and coordinating further steps, we have not encountered each other in a shared physical space, neither did our students. Such constant presence in virtual spaces and places allowed us to truly experience composing and interacting with the environment and looking at successful outcomes of such composing as dependent on both human competencies and capacities of non-human, material participants of the project. As English instructors, we wanted to explore the role of non-human elements in mediating transnational interactions. Facebook and Skype were chosen based on existing research in New Media Studies advocating for the use of participatory social media in telecollaborative international experience projects (Shuter). Our hopes were that social media and their interactive affordances would help us promote the development of intercultural communicative competencies among our students within and across their transnational groups (groups of students from different countries working together in the course of the project) and contribute to handling any issues or friction points that they may experience when communicating across time zones, languages, and national cultures.

While Boyle posed that "there is much pedagogical possibility in practicing within multiple composing environments (cell networks, intranets, mesh networks)", we lacked expertise in making decisions about the choice of virtual spaces for the ICP beyond widely known networked platforms (Boyle 543). Facebook and Skype were chosen as platforms familiar to all project participants with hopes to minimize learning curves that students have to overcome as part of the project. Both platforms have been heavily utilized by students in Russia and the U.S. at the start of the ICP for personal purposes, which we believed would allow for a quick and painless transfer of competencies with minimal time spent in class battling with technical issues.

In sequencing the assignments within the International Conference Project, we followed the principle of serial practice and constructed ICP of continuous items that are "distinct from one another without being separate" (Boyle 547). In alignment with key ideas of scholarly discussion about the goals of online writing in global contexts, we designed the ICP to unfold in three stages: "contact, convey, connect" (Amant and Rice). The table 7.1 illustrates each step, the assignments, and virtual platforms utilized at each step.

Since Ekaterina and the administration of the Russian Technical College decided to create an elective course for the sake of the ICP and enroll students interested in transnational inquiry initiative with broad communicative objectives, the process of the ICP was largely driven by the existing curriculum of the First-Year Writing Program (FYWP) at the college in the U.S. The existing FYWP curriculum engaged students in an Advanced Composition Class into a sequence of academic writing assignments culminating in a Research Project and an Argument Paper focused on developing a number of academic and professional competencies related to planning, developing, conducting, and presenting socially and personally relevant research. Since ICP was intended as a small-group collaborative transnational initiative, the existing curriculum was adapted to support the above format and expand the focus beyond national borders to reach wider audiences and encompass professional communicative competencies across nations and languages. Research topics, negotiated with ICP participants at the first stage of the project, were adapted to be of global impact and of interest to larger international audiences. As a result, the existing curriculum expanded to incorporate varied communicative tasks needed at all stages of professional communications remotely across borders: introductions, small group discussions, appropriate peer feedback sessions, interviews, and media presentations. At the same time, the number of graded assignments leading to the Research Project and the Argument Paper was reduced to support the goals of the ICP. Russian students were not required to write an Argument Paper relating their Research Findings. The ICP concluded with peer responses to the Video Presentations of Research shared on the FB group.

Table 7.1 The stages, elements, and tasks of the International Conference Project.

STAGE	PURPOSE	MEDIA	TASKS
Stage I	CONTACT	FACEBOOK GROUP	• Introductions and Responses • Discussion of Topics within Groups • Choosing relevant topics • Formulating Research Questions in Groups • Posting and Responding to Bibliographies within Groups • Posting Interview Questions
Stage II	CONVEY	SKYPE FACEBOOK CHAT	• Interviewing peers from a different country
Stage III	CONNECT	FACEBOOK GROUP SMARTPHONE (to record and share the videos) FACEBOOK CHAT ONLINE SURVEY	• Recording, posting, and responding to video presentations within and outside assigned groups • Project reflections via an anonymous survey

Ecological considerations are prominent when looking at the table presented above. Yagelski argues that "in school we teach separateness rather than interconnectedness; we see a world defined by duality rather than unity" (Yagelski 17). The ICP, on the contrary, resembles a continuous purposeful process of networked interactions between its participants, administrators, media platforms, media elements, and exchange and transfer of multiple human and non-human competencies to navigate professional transnational communicative reality. The International Conference Project engaged all of the elements of its ecology into uninterrupted process of production of content (administrators and students), communicative strategies (administrators, students, and media elements), and knowledge (all). This process equally engaged two instructors/administrators, social media platforms and their elements, and the students who remained constantly "plugged in" for the whole duration of the ICP. The process resembled a living ecology of interconnected and interdependent elements. Boyle explains that "rhetoric is an exercise of moving across biological, technical, and cultural registers" (551). The ICP allowed for the rhetoric to unfold and involved human and non-human project participants in a continuous process of problem-solving, decision making, and creation and application of resources and repertoires to make meaning across borders, time-zones, languages, cultures, rhetorics, and media.

Writing Makes Practice: Possibilities for Transnational Writing Projects and Pedagogies in English Education Curriculum at Four Year Colleges

When non-human elements, even those familiar to us in non-professional contexts, become rightful participants in a composition project and facilitate transnational interactions within it, an already complex transnational project becomes even less predictable.

Boyle argues:

"Posthumanism aids in rethinking practice as ecological, irreducible to an individual's agency. As networked media help facilitate and generate more of our interactions, we are becoming more practices in a betweenness and more sensitive to being in relation to an innumerable number of technological systems" (540).

Post-human practice tunes not only a writer to an ecology of media but the ecology itself (p. 543). In the course of the ICP, our classes became this continuous process of tuning and being tuned. It is important to point out that when live interaction in virtual spaces becomes part of composing for a class, the used-to-be controlled classroom environment turned into an "arena of social activity less controllable than classroom or other organized settings" (Thorne 144). It is hard for some of us to imagine being in charge of a class that we cannot fully control. Thorne argues, however, that such a practice presents compelling opportunities for agentive action and meaning making (144). From the perspectives of instructional design, such projects need to be thoroughly laid-out prior to being executed. Changes and adjustments will need to be made throughout the projects, and it cannot be often predicted when such changes will be necessary. For instance, we noticed that our students were not "contacting" well in the first stage of the process. Their introductory posts, even those accompanied by pictures, did not receive many comments and reactions. Students in most transnational groups did not take interactions further to a deeper level of interpersonal and group communication as the project progressed while a great number of them indicated in exit surveys that they hoped for pen-pal relationships with foreign groupmates. As a result, we had to reduce the time allocated to the contact phase and help our students start more meaningful focused discussions within assigned transnational groups. Similarly, looking at findings in International Education (Dooly, Clouet, etc.) we initially planned to allow all students to interview foreign peers via Skype to experience transformative results (overcome linguistic and cultural barriers, gain confidence as communicators, build relationships) (Shuter; George et al.). However, we came across the students' resistance to execute the above plan. As we discovered, Skype- real-time video conferencing tool- demanded from our students to truly "face" one another. Most students expressed to us that they did not feel ready for a more spontaneous contact for various reasons. Russian students were self-conscious with regards to their language abilities (which did not cause issues on FB). American students explained that they lacked pragmatics in knowing what to say, how to behave, etc. when communicating with foreigners and were not ready for Skype either. As a result, we made Skype interviews voluntary and converted most of the interviews to the FB chat, which allowed for both real-time and delayed interactions with no forced immediacy. Such various adjustments occurred at every stage of the ICP process, and, in some cases, demanded from us the instructors, to give students authority in decision making or trust non-human participants (FB and Skype) to "handle" interactions within certain project stages.

In light of the above, some may want to ask, what expertise should writing instructors possess when working on virtual projects with colleagues and students across borders? Although we read a great number of articles across disciplines to educate ourselves on potential challenges of the project, we often were not exactly prepared to handle the classes pedagogically. In simple terms, lesson plans do not work in practice-focused networked transnational collaborative initiatives. Instructors need to be prepared to handle issues being considered at any given time. Such issues may pertain to questions of cultural, rhetorical, or language differences; they may also deal with non-human aspects of transnational interactions: use of virtual spaces, capacities, affordances and hindrances such spaces and places bring with them into the classroom ecology. For instance, I walked into my classroom a number of times to be greeted with questions on issues emerging among our constantly "plugged-in" students in their transnational groups. Some issues related to rhetorical differences in virtual professional interactions between Russia and the U.S. For instance, some Russian students used formal, "Queen's English", in FB posts which alienated and, sometimes, offended their American peers. As a result, on a number of occasions I invited my students to share examples of "offensive" or alienating language they encountered as part of the ICP or when facing representatives of different cultures, national and domestic, on our vacation trips, visits of relatives, encounters at restaurants and cultural festivals, etc. Students shared their perceptions from such encounters and strategies they used to reduce negative outcomes in conversations with foreigners. I also contributed to such discussions bringing in systematic ways and methods to analyze and evaluate the reasons and motives behind such communication as well as material to help classify such reasons and apply appropriate repair strategies. I also shared my experiences with formal writing in Russia, addressing its cultural norms. At the same time, my colleague in Russia, Ekaterina, devoted a whole class period to the issue of tone of Russian students on FB and helping her students experiment with other, more informal, repertoires within the space of the project. Ekaterina and I constantly shared materials, ideas, issues raised in discussions with students, and activities by means of our FB chat.

The biggest friction point that Ekaterina dealt with on her side was her students' frustration that the ICP was taking more of a pragmatic and outcome-focused than a friendly turn that they had hoped for. Russian students seemed to believe that their American peers were too focused on "getting stuff done" and did not seem to be "interested in talking" to Russian peers. Ekaterina explained to me that she pulled out her lecture on cultural differences between Russia and the U.S. that she had delivered in her higher-level English courses to introduce to students the idea of cultural differences as they play out in various contexts: from personal to professional. For instance, using Geert's Hofstede website and theory on cultural dimensions, she discussed how cultures may be compared at national and organizational levels, what may cause difficulties when working with representatives of a different national culture. One of the dimensions relevant to the professional landscape that Hofstede compares at a national level is "individualism" (Hofstede). Russia is generally described as a collectivistic culture, while the U.S. is described as a more individualistic culture. Having unpacked each of the two societal structures, Ekaterina discussed with her students' potential implications of such differences for their encounters with American peers in the ICP. Russian students provided examples where they believed individualism caused issues of misunderstanding and misjudgment on their part in the course of the ICP. Such "unplanned" exercises and lectures that we often put together in a hurry using existing resources or by constantly reading, synthesizing, and exchanging relevant research excerpts immensely helped our students and ourselves develop competencies and strategies to succeed in virtual transnational interactions and in composing for global audiences.

As one can conclude from the above, virtual transnational projects designed with post-humanistic considerations at focus transform a traditional English classroom: they take the authority and control away from the instructors, "force" them to put trust into non-human elements to foster learning, and, most importantly, refuse instructors their "safe-zones"- pre-designed lessons plans to face the challenges of the professional writing in virtual spaces across borders, languages, and cultures as they unfold. Moreover, such instruction does not have an easily measured "end-goal" or set of outcomes easily pinpointed. While it is focused on the development of the Transnational Communicative Competencies in its cultural, linguistic, rhetorical, and spatial dimensions, the developmental process is much less controlled and depends on a number of variables which often cannot be predicted before the start of the initiative. Posthumanism accepts reciprocal tuning of people and things, posing challenges related to instructors, their readiness and motivation to face uncontrollable and to teach to the challenges of the "real" world. (Pickering 172).

Tele-collaborative Transnational Writing Pedagogies through Post-humanistic Lens: Goals and Learning Outcomes

While there is not and cannot be one teachable model of communicative competency, virtual transnational projects designed with post-humanistic considerations at heart are the future of instruction in writing and rhetoric and (when officially entered into college curricula) will require a description of learning outcomes. In many contemporary writing programs today, we teach students to acquire and navigate new and exciting repertoires: rhetorical, linguistic, cultural, and spatial, to succeed in communicating with various audiences across media and modes. As a result, students develop various competencies and strategies for their success in today's global professional communicative landscape. Cumulatively, such competencies are often assembled into a term "communicative" (British Council). Although intentionally vague, this term needed to be a bit more specified and well-defined for the sake of the International Conference Project. After careful considerations of existing research in Cultural Studies and Applied Linguistics, we formulated a number of important tenets:

a)   Networked transnational interactions occur along various communicative trajectories and require the development of competencies to navigate their cultural, linguistic, rhetorical, and spatial (non-human) dimensions.

b) Intercultural and/or socio-cultural competency commonly defined as "readiness and ability to sustain the dialogue of cultures" (Solovova) is extremely important to develop as a result of transnational collaborative projects at a college level. However, a more world-focused and clear definition needs to be formulated to cater to transnational encounters (oral and written) that occur remotely and are mediated by non-human participants: various participatory New Media at both personal and professional levels.

The Trajectories of Transnational Communicative Competencies

As a result, we formulated an umbrella term to identify the overarching goal of our project: the development of "transnational communicative competencies" (TCCs) along linguistic, cultural, rhetorical, and spatial trajectories. "Transnational communicative competencies" encompass an array of competencies, strategies, etc. that bring communication across borders and repertoires to desired success, however the success is defined by each party involved. We deliberately veered away from a singular noun "competency" in TCCs and switched to plural "competencies" since to be truly successful when interacting across languages, cultures, rhetorics, and media, students need to possess a number of communicative competencies. Further, to systematize and better facilitate the development of transnational communicative competencies among ICP participants, we outlined the targeted trajectories of such competencies. We wanted to work on devising ways to help our students better understand the notion of "culture" in its multiplicity and navigate in written communication, the national cultures of their peers, i.e. sustain the dialogue of national cultures. It was very important for us to help students explore rhetorical approaches and strategies in academic and research writing in Russia and the U.S. Finally, competencies to professionally communicate across linguistic differences and within New Media could not be disregarded in our project. As a result, four trajectories of TCCs emerged: cultural, rhetorical, linguistic and spatial (non-human).

When submitting the ICP proposal to our respective college administrators for approval, we outline the development of TCCs along its four trajectories as the end-goal of our project. It is important here to mention that we expected ICP to be nothing more than a process of such a development, potentially, without strictly measurable or clearly identifiable outcomes and proceeding at a pace individual to each participant. Below, we outline our conceptualization of each of the above trajectories in light of the ICP and professional networked transnational and global communications. Specifically, within each trajectory, we focus on competencies and strategies important to develop and possess to be a competent communicator in transnational settings.

The Cultural Trajectory

The cultural trajectory of transnational communicative competencies (TCCs) embraces variety and difference at a qualitatively new level. A key idea in most definitions of intercultural competency is the ability to sustain an "intercultural dialogue" requiring openness and empathy and resulting in a deep understanding of one another (Ganesh and Holmes). Further,

> "interculturally competent (ICC) speaker turns intercultural encounters into intercultural relationships—someone determined to understand, to gain an insider view of the other person's culture while also contributing to the other person's understanding of his/her own culture from an insider's point of view" (Byram "Teaching and Assesing" 34).

Meyer assembles the above definition into a set of social and communicative competencies that need to be developed in individuals involved in transnational interactions. Social competencies include working collaboratively, being flexible, dealing with conflicts, tolerating ambiguity, etc.; communicative ones are more pragmatic and include competencies in managing interactions, accepting and working with various speech styles, speeds, and patterns. Undeniably, an appreciation of the importance of various levels of culture (national, individual, group, identity, etc.) in transnational interactions is a necessary starting point in the development of TCCs along the cultural trajectory. As researchers in Cultural Studies agree, culture "operates at six levels" at least: national, organizational, identity, functional, team, and individual" (TMC). As a result, focusing on a national culture only when working/communicating transnationally may result in limited development of TCCs along the cultural trajectory and a distorted/stereotypical view of a national culture. When interacting across national borders, it is important to understand that certain communicative behaviors and rhetorical strategies may be unique not only to a specific national culture, but also the culture of a group or an organization a particular speaker belongs to, etc. As a result of the ICP, we wanted to develop culturally competent speakers able to work with and across differences without creating or reinforcing stereotypes. It is especially important to convey the complexity of the impact that culture, in its multiplicity, may have on an interlocutor's behavior expanding focus beyond a nationality as interlocutors "have the agency to move beyond their "native" cultures to reconstruct third cultures or new spaces for the negotiation of meaning" (*Translingual Practice* 78). With abundant research in intercultural competency, the process of its development as well as systems of measuring progress remain vaguely described. Most researchers argue that the key in assessing and facilitating the development of intercultural competency is the focus on process that is highly individual and variable. As for the measurements, the field of Cultural Studies gradually moves away from metrics-based assessments to open teacher-student assessment of the development of cultural competency or competencies and portfolio-based assessments that allow for guided self-reflection (Clouet).

The Linguistic Trajectory

Traditionally, the development of the cultural trajectory of TCCs is linked directly with the development of linguistic competency in a targeted language. Researchers in cultural studies believe that foreign language awareness is necessary to be successful (i.e. to achieve communicative goals) when communicating transnationally. English as a Second Language field is known for its focus on linguistic accuracy in contact zone interactions. When employees in sixty percent of U.S-based international companies have daily contact, direct or remote/networked, with colleagues, clients, partners and vendors overseas, an increasing number of Americans leave the U.S. to work abroad, as the popularity of remote transnational professional communications experiences exponential growth, accuracy in English or a foreign language is no longer the focus (Transitionabroad.com, the British Council). Communicators in the global reality do not need to accurately use a foreign language to successfully make meaning. Canagarajah argues that in diverse communicative contexts a new linguistic competency, more strategic than grammatical, is needed for success. He poses, that "what we need for contact zones is a competency that transcends individual languages, a translingual competency perhaps, that enables one to deal with the unpredictable mix of languages (*Translingual Practice* 69).

As a result, the focus on linguistic accuracy in transnational, global, diverse and networked communicative environments get replaced by a competency of managing available linguistic repertoires for the success of a transnational encounter. Linguistically competent global communicators are able to successfully apply various negotiation strategies to make meaning across languages. Canagarajah points out that, "paradoxically", those engaged in transnational encounters contract space "for acceptance of differences, not a sharedness", and, as a result, negotiate actively (*Translingual Practice* 82). Moreover, lexical and idiomatic differences can help achieve intelligibility and unlock curiosity and desire to make meaning across languages. What this means for those preparing to write or speak for global audiences is that accurate usage of English or a foreign language may not lead to success.

However, possessing skills of negotiating, asking, clarifying, pulling on various linguistic resources available, as well as a "cooperative disposition" with a focus on the desired outcome will (*Translingual Practice* 176). In his work, Pennycook affirms:

> "We are not in fact 'native speakers' of things called 'languages' so much as we engage in local language practices ... becoming a resourceful speaker is what we are surely aiming at, an idea that embraces both the ability to accommodate others and to manipulate different resources" (172).

The development of resourceful and strategic communicators able to regard all languages at hand as useful repertoires for meaning-making is what we were targeting as part of the ICP.

The Rhetorical Trajectory

To continue along the trajectories of TCCs, it is important to understand, especially in remote encounters that occur in writing, how thought and communicative patterns are shaped in professional discourses. Research in business negotiations across borders speaks to the above point. What place does humor have in business negotiations in China versus the U.S.? What stages are sales negotiations expected to have in Finland versus Norway? How much small talk is appropriate at the early stage of sales negotiations in the U.S. versus Germany? Researchers who studied rhetorical strategies and values of professional and business interactions specific to a genre and a national culture found that transnational encounters in high-stakes professional settings are successful when both parties are actively engaged in the pre-stage talks: conversations about their specific rhetorical repertoires and strategies within a given genre and negotiations around contradictions and controversies (Ardichivili et al.). Thus, despite cultural training provided to employees working in transnational teams, reciprocal dialogue of differences specific to a communicative task, context, and genre is necessary to succeed. With the above in mind, the International Conference Project assignments were sequenced to create the negotiation environment beyond a language and a national culture where students are motivated to create content and work through barriers, discomforts, perceptions and remain open to negotiate and learn from one another.

Spatial (non-human) Trajectory

When transnational encounters are predominately written and face-to-face contact with all its affordances is minimized, all resources at hand are important to utilize to succeed. Pennycook argues that language practices can no longer be studied in isolation from places where they occur. The researcher suggests that a communication act across languages is possible not only due to the resources, repertoires, and competencies that humans bring forth, but largely to material resources that certain places make available to humans in such interactions (165). Also, of great importance to translingual and transnational interactions are the relations between individuals and spatial resources (resources provided by and in the context of interactions) and how various spatial material resources become part of human competencies to successfully navigate transnational encounters (Blommaert and Backus 26). Boyle and others point out that a vast majority of transnational encounters occur in virtual places and spaces. Today we *translanguage* in multiple composing environments (cell networks, intranets, mesh networks), and bringing those to a composition class for practice is extremely important (Boyle). In networked interactions human competencies alone may not do the trick; it is important to properly choose media participants (social networks, communities, video-conference platforms, etc.) and consider the competencies and affordances of these non-human participants of transnational encounters. For instance, as the ICP proceeded, we discovered that Facebook with its emphasis on community building lacks competencies for professional interactions: file-sharing, enhanced communicative support, time-zone difference facilitation, interactivity, etc. Moreover, by making Facebook the primary interaction space, we created an initial impression that ICP is more of a pen-pal, chat-style endeavor rather than a professional research activity to be put on students' resumes. ICP demonstrated that English faculty need training to better understand the purposes and affordances of existing New Media as well as expertise in aligning the media with the goals of their projects in sound professional ways. Therefore, the spatial trajectory of TCCs that involves material repertoires and resources provided by the places and spaces where interactions occur and our facility and relationships with those resources and repertoires cannot be overlooked in tele-collaborative projects.

To sum up, in order to develop competencies to successfully communicate in transnational settings, all parties need to be ready to step into a continuous process of working on attitudes, knowledge, skills and strategies aimed at becoming aware and being able to negotiate meaning across linguistic, cultural, rhetorical barriers recognizing, using, and building spatial repertoires. As Deardorff points out, such a journey can be entered in at any time and is never-ending as the learner continues to learn, change, evolve, and become transformed with time "honing and gaining greater clarity of one's position in relation to an exterior object (or skill)" (Deardorff, Boyle 546). Teaching towards TCCs along the four trajectories requires a "willingness to consider new ways of being and thinking in the world" (*The Framework* 541).

English faculty and administration need to consider that in the global professional world "rhetoric becomes an art of connectivity and thereby asks for new considerations from multiple angles that engage multiple fields" (539). In light of the above, even with identified trajectories of TCCs, teaching to write and communicate across borders, languages, cultures, and with spatial repertoires requires us to re-imagine not only the process of learning, but also the teaching process as continuous practice in and among the unexplored. Considering our space limitations in this manuscript and a decent amount of existing knowledge base along the first three trajectories of TCCs, we would like to devote the remaining section of our chapter to the non-human. We believe that the least explored among TCCs trajectories is currently the spatial one. Therefore, we intend to share our appreciation for the material of the ICP: Facebook and Skype. Most importantly, we would like to share our findings, bibliographic and practical, as they pertain to the affordances of New Media for transnational collaborative classroom-based projects and considerations for the choice of specific social media to promote TCCs in projects like ICP.

Works Cited

Amant, Kirk St., and Rich Rice. "Online Writing in Global Contexts: Rethinking the Nature of Connections and Communication in the Age of International Online Media". Computers and Composition, vol. 38, 2015, pp. 113-176.

Ardichvili, A., et al. "A Theory of Entrepreneurial Opportunity Identification and Development," *Journal of Business Venturing,* vol. 18, no. 1, 2003, pp. 105-123.

Association of American Colleges and Universities (AAC&U). "College Students are More Diverse than Ever." *AAC&U News.* 2019, aacu.org. Accessed March 2020.

Blommaert, Jan., and Ad Backus. "Superdiverse Repertoires and the Individual." *Multilingualism and Multimodality: Current Challenges for Educational Studies,* edited by Ingrid de Saint-Georges and Jean-Jacques Weber, SensePublishers, 2013, pp. 11–32.

Boyd, Danah., and Nicole Ellison. "Social Network Sites: Definition, History, and Scholarship". *Journal of Computer-Mediated Communication,* 2007, *no.* 13, vol 1, pp. 210–230.

Boyle, Casey. "Writing and Rhetoric and/as Posthuman Practice", *College English,* 2016, vol.71, no. 6, pp. 532-554.

British Council. "Culture at Work: The Value of Intercultural Skills in the Workplace". *Policy Insight and Research,* 2013, https://www.britishcouncil. org/. Accessed March 2019.

Byram, Michael. *Teaching and Assessing Intercultural Communicative Competence.* Multilingual Matters, 1997.

—. "Instrumental and Educational Dimensions of Intercultural Communication." *Stylistics and Theory of Language Communication: conf.,* Moscow, 2005.

Canagarajah, Suresh. "Codemeshing in Academic Writing: Identifying Teachable Strategies of Translanguaging". *The Modern Language Journal*, vol. 95, 2011, pp. 401–417.

—. "Translingual Practice: Global Englishes and Cosmopolitan Relations." Routledge. 2013.

"Career Readiness Defined". *National Association of Colleges and Employers*, naceweb.org. Accessed March 2020.

Clouet, Richard. "Understanding and Assessing Intercultural Competency in an Online Environment: A Case Study, *RESLA*, 2013, vol. 26, pp. 139-157.

Cooper, Marilyn. "Being Linked to the Matrix: Biology, Technology, and Writing." *Rhetorics and Technologies: New Directions in Writing and Communication* Ed. Stuart Selber. Columbia: University of South Carolina, 2010, pp. 15–32.

Council of Writing Program Administrators, National Council of Teachers of English, and National Writing Project. "Framework for Success in Postsecondary Writing." 2011, *WPA Council*, http://wpacouncil.org/. Accessed April 2019.

Deardorff, Darla. "Identification and Assessment of Intercultural Competency as a Student Outcome of Internationalization". Journal of Studies in International Education, 2006, vol. 10, no.3, pp. 241-266.

Dooly, M. "Crossing the Intercultural Borders into 3rd Space Culture(s): Implications for Teacher Education in the Twenty-First Century." *Language & Intercultural Communication*, 2011, vol. *11, no.* 4, pp. 319-337.

Frey, Willia."The Millennial Generation: A Demographic Bridge to America's Diverse Future". *The Brookings Institution, 2019*, brookings.com. Accessed March 2020.

Ganesh, Shiv., and Prue Holmes. "Positioning Intercultural Dialogue—Theories, Pragmatics, and an Agenda". Journal of International and Intercultural Communication, 2011, voil.4, no.2, pp. 81-86.

George, Daniel., et al. "Use of Social Media in Graduate-Level Medical Humanities Education: Two Pilot Studies from Penn State College of Medicine". *MedTech*, 2011, vol. 33, no. 8, pp. 429-434.

"Global Enterprise Forecast". *PRNewswire*, 23 September 2019, prnewswire.com. Accessed March 2020.

Herbrechter, Stefan. *Posthumanism: A Critical Analysis*. Bloomsbury Academic, 2013.

Hofstede, Geert. *Culture's Consequences: Comparing Values, Behaviors, Institutions and Organizations across Nations*. Thousand Oaks, 2001.

"Job Outlook Survey". *National Association of Colleges and Employers, 2017-2019*, naceweb.org. Accessed March 2020.

Kaplan, Robert. Cultural Thought Patterns in Inter-cultural Education. *Language Learning*, no.16, 1996, pp. 1-20.

Karnyashev, A.D., et al. "College Students' Intercultural Competency and Interethnic Tolerance". *Russian Education and Society*, 2014, vol. 56 no. 9, pp. 3–26.

Lenhart, Amanda. "Teens, Social Media & Technology Overview 2015". *Pew Research Center: Internet, Science & Tech*, April, 2015.

Lewis, Sarah., Pea, Roy, and Rosen, Joseph. "Beyond Participation to Co-Creation of Meaning: Mobile Social Media in Generative Learning Communities". *Social Science Information, 2010, vol.,* 49, no.3.

McEwan, Bree., and Miriam Sobre-Denton. "Virtual Cosmopolitanism: Constructing Third Cultures and Transmitting Social and Cultural Capital Through Social Media". *Journal of International and Intercultural Communication,* 2011, vol. 4, no. 4, pp. 252-258.

McNeill, L. "There is no "I" in network: Social networking sites and post-human autobiography." *Biography,* 2012, vol. 35, no.1, pp. 65–82.

Paran, Amos., and Lies Sercu. *Testing the Untestable in Language Education,* 2010 Clevedon: Multlingual Matters.

Pennycook, Alastair. "Translanguaging and Semiotic Assemblages". *International Journal of Multilingualism,* 2017, vol. 12, no. 4, pp. 269-282.

Perry, Mark. "Large US firms Sell, Hire and Invest More Overseas than in US and They Have to Think Globally to Survive". *American Enterprise Institute, 2016,* ael.org. Accessed March 2020.

Pickering, Andrew. "Practice and Posthumanism." *The Practice Turn in Contemporary Theory,* Ed. Theodore Schatzki. New York: Routledge, 2001, pp.163-74.

Schreiber, Brooke. "I am what I am: Multilingual Identity and Digital Translanguaging". *Language Learning & Technology,* 2015, vol. 19, no. 3, pp. 69-87.

Shuter, Robert. "Introduction: New media Across Cultures—Prospect and Promise". *Journal of International & Intercultural Communication,* 2011, vol., 4, no. 4, pp. 241-245.

—. "Intercultural New Media studies: The Next Frontier in Intercultural Communication". *Journal of Intercultural Communication Research,* 2012, vol. 41, no. 3, pp. 219-237.

Solovova, Elena. "Methodology of English Language Teaching". Moscow. AST: Astrel. Poligraphizdat.

Starosta, W., and A. Olorunnisola. "A Meta-Model for Third Culture Development". Paper presented at the annual convention of Eastern Communication Association. 4 April 1995, Pittsburgh, PA.

Thorne, Steven. "The 'Intercultural Turn' and Language Learning in the Crucible of New Media". In F. Helm and S. Guth (Eds.), *Telecollaboration 2.0 for Language and Intercultural Learning, 2010,* pp. 139-164, Bern: Peter Lang.

TMC. "Six Levels of Culture". *Cultural Orientations Approach.* Tmcorp.com. Accessed March 2019.

Tuleja, Elizabeth. "Developing Cultural Intelligence for Global Leadership through Mindfulness". J*ournal of Teaching in International Business,* 2014, vol. 25, pp. 5-24.

Yagelski, Robert. "Writing as a Way of Being: Writing Instruction, Nonduality, and the Crisis of Sustainability". 2001. Cresskill. Hampton Press.

Chapter 8

Investigating Translingual Practices in First-Year Writing Courses: Implications for Transnational Composition Pedagogies

Phuong M. Tran, Kyle Lucas, and Kenny Tanemura

Purdue University

Abstract: Institutions of higher education in the U.S continue to undergo an internationalization process which has manifested in different forms of administration: in increasing recruitment of international students to US campuses (Rose and Weiser 3), in the establishment of international campuses and facilities beyond the country's borders, or in partnerships with universities and academic programs all over the world (Martins 2). The internationalization of US writing programs has kindled academic discourse on transnational composition, and in recent years, writing scholars, administrators, and instructors have been discussing the need for pedagogical ideologies and practices that will serve transnational composition contexts, one of which is translingual pedagogy (Canaragajah 33; You 6). This chapter joins in the conversation about the translingualism-transnationalism relations by situating translingual writing as a pedagogical approach in transnational first-year composition. The chapter investigates the following question: Why and how are translingual practices viable pedagogical interventions for transnational first-year composition courses? We begin by reviewing the existing scholarship on first-year writing courses that adopted translingual approaches to examine the demographic and pedagogical configuration of these courses. We proceed by reporting the findings of our inquiry, detailing the context, student makeup, pedagogical objectives, and assignments and activities in the reviewed courses. We conclude by discussing the contribution of translingual approaches to transnational composition pedagogies as well as implications for future directions.

Keywords: transnational composition, transnational composition pedagogy, translingual writing, translingual writing pedagogy, translingualism, writing program internationalization, first-year writing pedagogy

***

Institutions of higher education in the U.S continue to undergo an internationalization process. At many institutions, this process has manifested itself in different forms of administration: in increasing recruitment of international students to US campuses (Rose and Weiser 3), in the establishment of international campuses and facilities beyond the country's borders, or in partnerships with universities and academic programs all over the world (Martins 2). The immediate results of internationalization can be witnessed in both US institutions' physical spaces and virtual territories. While recruitment for diversity has brought a steady rise of international students to US universities and colleges for the past ten consecutive years (Institute of International Education), this agenda has also connected US domestic students with peers around the world via transnational programs. In both ways, internationalization has expanded the already multicultural and multilingual student demographics of US institutions to various dimensions, putting all students into a situation of "[linguistic and cultural] super-diversity" (Vertovec 1025).

The internationalization of US writing programs has kindled academic discourse on transnational composition since the early 2010s. Starting out with discussions about the increasing enrollment of international students in US-based writing programs, this discourse has gradually expanded to address WPA work in cross-institutional contexts, where writing programs in American universities collaborate with similar programs in a university's international branch campus (Donahue, "Internationalization" 212). David Martins' book, *Transnational Writing Program Administration*, published in 2015, is a seminal text that officially cemented the scholarship of transnational composition, paving the way for more fruitful and rigorous conversations about this area. In recent years, writing scholars, administrators, and instructors have been discussing the need for pedagogical ideologies and practices that will serve transnational composition contexts, one of which is translingual pedagogy.

In the last decade, translingualism has emerged as "an intellectual movement" (Matsuda 478) that proposes a new paradigm in language teaching, capitalizing on students' multilingual, multicultural repertoires in composing (Horner et al.). Starting with the resistance and confrontation towards the traditional monolingual paradigm that privileges Standard

American English (Horner and Trimbur; Horner and Lu), translingual scholars have been challenging static linguistic norms and promoting a view of languages as fluid and in constant change rather than discrete (Canagarajah, "Negotiating"). Perceiving language differences as a new "norm" (Lu and Horner) and as resources rather than deficits (Horner et al.), translingual scholars advocate for the negotiation of meaning between users of diverse linguistic and cultural backgrounds to achieve a more agentive use of language and dynamic construction of identity (Canagarajah, "Negotiating"). When translated into classroom practices, translingualism has received both compliments and reservations. Proponents of this approach point out its several benefits to multilingual, multicultural students. Translingual pedagogies are said to attend to these students' communicative purposes, engage them in language and cultural difference, and enable them to utilize their diverse linguistic and cultural resources in meaning-making (Martín et al. 144). These pedagogies also sharpen students' rhetorical and intercultural sensitivity (see Guerra), give them agency and voice in composing processes (Tardy 181), and provide them with a dynamic composing platform responsive to a globalized, mobilized, and rapidly changing world (Martín et al. 144). Some scholars in related fields, on the other hand, lament on the shortage in translingual scholarship that assists language acquisition and proficiency development in language learners (see Atkinson et al.; Shawna Shapiro et al.). Despite these critiques, scholarly discussion has been initiated about the compatibility between translingual pedagogies and transnational composition classrooms. Canagarajah argues that translingualism is most strongly correlated with writers in "liminal spaces" (spaces "between communities, languages, and nations") and as a result, these writers are led to "search for identities and literacies that go beyond bounded, static, and territorialized constructs and norms". To him, these "liminal spaces" are *transnational* (You 33). Xiao You sees translingualism, together with transculturalism and cosmopolitanism, as "the theoretical pillars of transnational writing education" (6). Finally, the common ground between translingual composition and transnational composition, as Carrie Kilfoil analyzes, lies in their engagement in "very deliberate and visible cross-language work and/or involve analysis of literacy practices ... in the context of increasing sociocultural diversity in higher education". The conversation on the seemingly inherent connections between translingualism as pedagogical approaches and transnational composition have been further invigorated in *Composition Studies*, Volume 44 Issue 1 in 2016.

This chapter joins in the conversation about the translingualism-transnationalism relations by situating translingual writing as a pedagogical approach in transnational first-year composition. The chapter investigates the following question: *Why and how are translingual practices viable pedagogical interventions for transnational first-year composition courses?* We begin by reviewing the existing scholarship on first-year writing courses that adopted translingual approaches to examine the demographic and pedagogical configuration of these courses. We proceed by reporting the findings of our inquiry, detailing the context, student makeup, pedagogical objectives, and assignments and activities in the reviewed courses. We conclude by discussing the contribution of translingual approaches to transnational composition pedagogies as well as implications for future directions.

Methodology

Terminology

Before investigating translingual pedagogies, it is necessary that we clarify key terminology to provide a coherent understanding of certain concepts explored in our research.

As David Martins states, the term "transnational" "can mean many different things" (3). Martins views transnational writing program administration in three dimensions – transnational positioning, transnational language, and transnational engagement, indicating the multifaceted, dynamic and emergent nature of conceptualizing transnational composition. In this chapter, we follow Canagarajah's definition of "transnational" as relations that go beyond the confines of nation-state boundaries (42). "Transnational composition", then, involves writers and writing practices that transcend such boundaries. More broadly, transnational composition can be situated within transnational writing education, which You defines as "efforts made to enable students to recognize, negotiate with, deconstruct, and transcend these boundaries (national, ethnic, racial, and linguistic) in the teaching of writing, ultimately cultivating flexible and responsible global citizens" (2). In this context, "transnational writers" can be understood as students participating in a transnational composition classroom. As such, transnational writers are not limited to nonnative speakers of English or multilingual students but also include native speakers or monolingual students in the traditional meaning of these terms. Being positioned in the transnational composition context promoting writing practices that transcend nation-state boundaries, all students become transnational writers as they engage in assignments and activities that require the act of crossing national borders physically (e.g., in partnership programs) and/or figuratively (e.g., in translation assignments).

In this paper, we specifically explore these assignments and activities within the context of a first-year writing course. The concept of "a first-year writing course" is tentatively defined as a composition course that (a) is labelled as "first-year writing", "freshman composition", or "introductory composition", (b) is run by an educational institution either in the US or abroad, and (c) is taken by students as part of their academic degree. We are particularly interested in how translingual pedagogy is applied in first-year writing courses.

The concept of "translingual pedagogy" should be comprehended in a flexible, inclusive fashion. In recent years, as pointed out by Zhaozhe Wang, the term "translingualism" as a movement has "experienced a neologistic 'identity crisis'" as it has been used interchangeably with different "derivative notions" such as "translingual orientation", "translingual literacies", "translingual practice", and "translingual approach". Therefore, "translingual pedagogy" in this chapter encompasses the pedagogical orientations, practices, and approaches that (a) instructors adopted for their first-year writing courses and that (b) they determined as "translingual."

Locating Relevant Scholarship

To locate the literature relevant to our research focus, we only selected and reviewed publications on first-year writing (FYW) courses where the instructor intentionally implemented translingual interventions in classroom activities and course assignments. That means we excluded from our review the following literature:

1. Publications on translingual pedagogy in other types of courses, such as basic writing, writing courses at higher levels than first year, graduate courses, or practicum courses.

2. Publications that offer pedagogical implications without any application in any specific first-year writing course (e.g., Chen).

3. Publications that use translingualism and/or translingual writing as a theoretical framework to investigate translingual features of student writing or the translingual identity of students without any implementation of a translingual pedagogy by the instructor.

This sampling approach enabled us to identify 13 relevant publications, including six academic journal articles, five chapters from edited collections, and two books. Mentioned in these publications is the projection of FYW courses that employed a translingual approach as identified by the instructor/author together with the instructor's testimonial about how they implemented one or more translingual interventions in their course. However, the number of courses in this scholarship is unidentifiable, as one publication can discuss multiple courses without specifying how many (e.g., De Costa et al.).

Coding Procedures

The selected publications were then read and coded separately by all three researchers for different aspects of course configuration, including:

- The context/location in which the course took place (US/Non-US/Transnational);

- Demographics of students (domestic [majority/minority]/international/mix);

- The pedagogical objective(s) that the course aimed to accomplish;

- The teaching practices employed in the course, namely, course assignments, classroom activities, and teaching materials.

After completing individual coding, we compared our results, discussed and resolved any discrepancies.

Findings

The literature under review indicates that several FYW courses have been described as adopting a translingual pedagogy. These courses took place in different contexts, were enrolled by students of diverse linguistic and socio-cultural backgrounds, addressed various pedagogical objectives, and employed a wide range of assignments and teaching materials.

With regards to context, 12 out of 13 reviewed publications discuss FYW courses that took place in the US (e.g., Kiernan et al. 3; Dryer and Mitchell 135). Courses held in non-US contexts were also reported, such as those in Lebanon (Ayash, "Toward" 63). Jerry Lee and Christopher Jenks recounted their experiences creating "an online classroom partnership between a US-based composition course ... and a similar course delivered in Hong Kong" (325), indicating that these courses were operating in a transnational context.

The linguistic demographics of students enrolled in the reviewed FYW with a translingual orientation was diverse. Five of the selected articles had a mix of native and nonnative speakers of English (e.g., Ayash, "Toward" 148; Lee and Jenks 324). The selected scholarship also includes courses attended by only domestic students (e.g., Liao 747) or only international students of different L1s in the US (e.g., Kiernan et al. 5). However, Lee emphasizes that domestic students in her study came from diverse linguistic backgrounds and at least a few students in every class used African American Language (319). Additionally, Ayash reported on FYW courses held in Lebanon, an EFL context, where students came from different first and second language backgrounds ("Toward" 78).

Regarding pedagogical objectives, one translingual course could embrace more than one objective. The pedagogical objectives pursued by the courses under study include:

- To raise students' awareness of their linguistic and cultural resources (e.g., Canagarajah, "Transnational" 139)

- To raise students' awareness of the linguistic and cultural politics and dynamics in a multilingual and multicultural society (e.g., Hanson 207)

- To raise students' awareness of their writer's identity and agency (e.g., Sohan 193)

- To sharpen students' rhetorical sensibility (e.g., Lueck and Sharma)

- To encourage students to explore cross-language relations and negotiate language differences in multilingual and multicultural spaces (e.g., Liao 743)

- To develop students' intercultural sensitivity (e.g., Lee and Jenks 325)

- To raise students' awareness of the impacts of the writing ecology on their composing process (e.g., De Costa et al. 468)

- To enhance students' digital literacies (e.g., Lee 321)

- To challenge the students' assumptions about language, life, and society (e.g., Gallagher and Noonan 174)

- To encourage students to challenge the monolingualist ideology (e.g.; Horner 95)

- To promote a translingual disposition towards linguistic diversity (e.g., Liao 758)

When it comes to teaching practices, the selected literature was coded for the assignments implemented in the reviewed FYW classrooms. We summarize the types of assignments that emerged from the review in what follows.

Translation Assignments

Translation is the most prevalent type of assignment in the reviewed scholarship. Kiernan et al. propose a translation assignment that "invites students to individually and collectively translate cultural texts from home languages into the shared English lingua franca of the U.S. writing classroom" (2) in order for them to realize how "comparison and reflection" intrinsic to translation is integral to reading and writing. Students go through three steps of translation: 1) "individual translation", where cultural texts are translated from the home language into English; 2) "group comparison and reflection", where students discuss their own and their classmates' translation and translation process; and (3) "individual reflection", where students reflect upon differences between their own and their peers' translations for developing "metalinguistic and metacognitive awareness" (6). Joleen Hanson designs another translation assignment, which requires students to find and translate a non-English website as part of their research. The goal of this assignment was two-fold: 1) to help students access "information or perspectives about their research topics that might not be available on English-language websites" and 2) "to engage students in negotiating language difference and to uproot the notion that a native-like fluency in another language is needed in order to use it" (209).

To counter deficit models, salute other languages and cultures as pedagogical resources, and capitalize on students' linguistic and cultural repertoires, Steven Fraiberg has his students introduce "key terms and concepts from their home cultures" (De Costa et al. 469). In this assignment, the students completed four tasks: (a) present the history of the term, (b) cite examples of its usage, c) compare the term with other related terms, and (d) analyze how the term signifies in the broader culture (469). The discussion about terms, as Fraiberg argues, can enrich students' knowledge of the "dynamic, material, contested, and socially situated" nature of language. At the same time, the activity places students in the expert position and celebrates their linguistic and cultural repertoires as "powerful resources for teaching and learning" (469).

Bruce Horner employs what he calls a "double translation activity", in which students select terms/phrases related to their work/identities (e.g., education, learning, and teaching) and translate them by referring to three different kinds of dictionaries: (a) any dictionary that provides a more or less literal definition of the term; (b) the Oxford English dictionary to gain "a history of the origins, different versions, uses, and meanings of the term over time"; and (c) a translation dictionary that "offers multiple ways of translating the term...into a language other than English" with consultations from native speakers (93). Students then write an essay explaining the different results from the three steps, justifying why writers would "choose one or another definition". By suggesting the multiple ways of "translating any one term into another language" instead of "treating languages as equivalent to stable 'code'", this assignment stresses the fluid and collaborative nature of languages and subverts monolingualist ideology (94)

Ayash promotes Critical Translation as a translingualism-oriented writing pedagogy, which is distinguished from traditional, monolingualist practices in grammar-translation methods. She introduces a writing-translation assignment sequence aimed at sharpening students' rhetorical savviness in processing and creating texts ("Toward" 140). The first assignment, (Re)writing Academic Tensions, asked students to revisit their previous academic writings and reflect on "difficult, unsatisfactory or unnatural" writing moments due to uneasy writerly feelings or obstructed meaning-making (150). Students rewrote/translated these "instances of dissonance or inauthenticity" to reconcile their writing with the existing writing purposes and intended meaning. Later, in the second assignment, Writer-Translator's Commentary, students rationalized their translation choices with supporting evidence from their revised/rewritten work and articulated how their translation triggered different meanings or understandings. The last assignment in the sequence, Meso-politics of Translation amid Reader Expectations, prompted students to consider the potential readership of their translations with regards to the "readability and intelligibility" of the work. Subsequently, students learned to scrutinize "the promise, stakes, and problematics of translations" in the relation between "their actual and imagined personal, civic, academic and professional life and work" (151).

The above translation assignments illustrate pedagogical attempts in teaching students how to challenge monolingualism/mono-nationalism. Conventional translation endorses this orientation by asking the translator to "[find] equivalents in meaning and form in two languages", which essentially is a search for "sameness" and a view of language difference only at the surface level (Horner and Tetreault 14). Translingual translation, in contrast, places students in a process, "a site of struggle" (19), where they constantly work and negotiate with language difference across time and space as they shuttle between communicative contexts. These assignments push students to find a difference in the meaning of the same text as they move from one language to another (Hanson), one type of dictionary to another (Horner), one culture to another (De Costa et al.), the EFL classroom in their home countries to the English lingua franca classroom in the US (Kiernan et al.), or one moment of writing to another (Ayash). In these assignments, students were required to recognize and utilize their various linguistic and cultural resources in communication, acknowledge and grapple with their counterparts' dissimilar resources, and always reflect on how language and meaning are reproduced in the shifting of context. In doing so, translingual translation assignments move students to a translingual/transnational orientation.

Reading Responses

Another common assignment was reading responses, which require students to read and respond to texts that deal with or highlight translingual-related themes and issues. For example, Vanessa Sohan suggests using *relocalized listening* as a reading response that cultivates translingual dispositions towards language conventions and language difference. As the author notes, this practice involves "ways of reading-writing-thinking that highlight the need of language users to relocalize established conventions in light of users' spatiotemporal contexts" (193). To foster the development of this practice, Sohan had students read Gloria Anzaldúa's "How to Tame a Wild Tongue" and locate a part (e.g., a phrase or passage) that stood out to them as strange or disconcerting. Students then analyzed their reaction to the text in a two-page essay, specifically focusing on why this reaction might be related to their views and beliefs as readers. In another reading response assignment, Lee required students to examine the advantages and disadvantages of code-meshed discourse, such as Vershawn Young's *Your Average Nigga* (324). The author argues that response-questions can be built around such readings for either writing prompts or classroom discussions. For instance, instructors could raise the question of "how code-meshing can be used to reinforce the meaning of a text in much the same way that illustrations supplement the meaning of a text in storybooks or music supplements the emotional sensations elicited by movie scenes" (342). A final example from Esther Milu discusses the use of critical reading responses, in which students examine "how their colonial histories had influenced their linguistic, cultural and ethnic identities" (De Costa et al. 467). In summary, reading responses can challenge monolingual assumptions about language by drawing attention to how texts are code-meshed (i.e., they are not composed using a single, standard language variety) and by having students critically reflect upon their reactions to such texts (i.e., if one is confused or disconcerted, why? And how can code-meshing be an effective rhetorical device to employ in writing?).

Literacy Narrative and Autoethnography

Literacy narrative was used as a genre to enact translingual writing in Suresh Canagarajah's, Ayash's, Liao's and Lee's and Jenks' FYW courses. In these contexts, students completed a literacy narrative recounting their experiences in language and literacy learning and development. Ayash's students profiled what language and literate affordances they could access within and beyond academic settings and how these affordances affected their own self-perception, ongoing literate work, and bonding with related individuals and social institutions ("Toward" 151). The students in Canagarajah's course conducted both secondary research through relevant readings and primary research through collecting data and documenting literacy artifacts revolving around their literacy development. Students were then allowed to exhibit their deliverables in a spectrum, from "a simple personal narrative on their language and literacy development" to a "well-researched autoethnography" (142). Finally, Lee and Jenks designed a Critical Literacy Narrative with a transnational and collaborative element, which we will detail in Pair/Collaborative Projects.

Also in the vein of autoethnographic assignments, Fang-yu Liao designed a Poetic Autoethnography project to enact translingual pedagogy through poetry writing. Spanning over six weeks, the project required each student to prepare a 12 to 20-page poetry book on their chosen topic. The poetry book was to consist of 10 poems that they wrote accompanied by an introduction and a conclusion reflecting on their writing experience. Later, students shared their poems and reflections in a five-minute presentation in class. Throughout the weeks, the instructor used sample poems written by former students, conducted poetry writing activities and classroom discussions, introduced and negotiated a grading criteria with students, and held three writing workshops on sensory words, sound poems, and collage poems. The project was an attempt to use poetry writing to develop a translingual disposition towards linguistic diversity in monolingual, domestic students (758).

In the literacy narrative/autoethnography assignments above, the act of recounting past experiences in literacy development, the self-discovery and the writing itself, be it in narrative or poetry, and the investigating process has moved students past monolingual/mono-transnational orientations. By revisiting their literacy development journey, students were able to remember and reinvigorate their various linguistic and cultural resources which turned out to be affordances for their writing. This is where their diverse repertoires were built up and enhanced. Students were also educated about how their composing processes and choices are always affected by the related communities (Canagarajah 122) and the surrounding political, socio-cultural ecology (Lee and Jenks, 337; Ayash 171) and recognized the limitations and insufficiency of monolingualism in reflecting language use and meaning. These literacy narrative assignments also advance a translingual disposition via their multimodal nature: students were allowed to mesh various linguistic, semiotic and cultural codes to exhibit their work at their disposal (e.g., Lee and Jenks 329), thus learnt to rhetorically reflect on and appreciate the values of diverse resources.

Multimodality and Multimedia

Four publications document multimodal and multimedia assignments as ways of implementing a translingual pedagogy. Melissa Lee discusses using digital literacy narratives to help students "explore the blurry and shifting boundaries between contextual ideas of standard and nonstandard, and discreteness versus fluidity" (321). By having students compose literacy narratives through audio or visual modes, Lee argues that students are allowed to use non-standard dialects and code-mesh while producing their work. In another assignment type, Xiqiao Wang had students complete a writing theory cartoon in order to tap into their visualization skills (De Costa et al. 468). Students in her class reflected on their negotiations with translingual and transnational experiences through drawing and constructing "visual metaphors" that present the processes, spaces, and experiences in which these negotiations occurred. These drawings, she argues, "reveal the material, cognitive, and affective dimensions of their multilingual experiences" (468).

Another multimodal assignment developed by Lueck and Sharma had students create closed captions for a film (*Raising Arizona*) that included non-prestigious dialects. Students were required to submit their captions on a class discussion forum, which was used to highlight differences in how the captions were created. As the authors note, this assignment aimed to help students understand the rhetorical decisions involved in transcription, especially those related to voice and identity.

Finally, using an *ePortfolio* tool, students in Gallagher and Noonan's course created multimodal compositions based on the following writing prompt: "I want you to experiment with the limits of language to bring this place to life for your reader. I want you to use the language descriptively. Build from what you know. What are the stories and places (and the people) that have shaped you?" (174). As a model, students read Susan Griffin's essay "Our Secret" and discussed how Griffin "collages together multiple discourses", changes in her style, diction, and voice throughout the essay and the "consequences of these choices" (175). This activity stresses how translingual practices can emerge from reading and writing activities, which subsequently develop translingual dispositions in students.

In summary, these assignments challenge the assumption that there is a monolithic, standard academic form of writing that must be employed in order to be rhetorically effective. Such activities highlight how language use is dynamic and ripe with variation across different media and modes.

Pair/Collaborative Projects

Two publications detail FYW courses where instructors purposefully arranged for native and nonnative speakers of English to collaborate in paired translingual assignments. Dryer and Mitchell's course enrolled both US domestic and international students, and course assignments, ranging from peer interviews to peer portfolio reviews, consistently required students to work with peers from other language and cultural backgrounds inside and outside of the classroom (143). Lee and Jenks discuss a transnational and digital context where a composition course in the US partnered with a similar course in Hong Kong. Students co-wrote drafts and gave others written comments in a Google Doc. The central assignment was a Critical Literacy Narrative, for which all students (i) examined their identity in a second language; (ii) read and responded to the writing of their international peers; and (iii) reflected in an essay on the whole cross-cultural learning experience (327). Students were allowed to narrativize their literacy experiences in their first language as well as non-language related activities.

These paired assignments, as the authors explain, are the means for them to initiate and develop a "translingual disposition" in students as a learning outcome. Pairing L1 and multilingual students together not only allowed increased cross-cultural, cross-linguistic interactions between two student groups but also put them in a space where they had to examine and adjust their own assumptions about language and culture. Through working with peers from other countries, students in these courses further understood the "complex and adaptive" nature of their English language and how socio-cultural factors influence one's literacy practices.

Discussion

As David S. Martins points out, transnational writing program administration involves "students and faculty from two or more countries working together and highlights the situated practices of such efforts" (2). The internationalization movement of US higher education has steadily and increasingly brought international students to US-based campuses and connected domestic students with peers in institutions around the world (1), making transnationalilty an integral part of US academic programs and classrooms, first-year writing included. Transnational spaces not only exist in partnership writing programs between institutions located in different countries but indeed are well-present in US-based writing courses where international undergraduates are matriculated either to mainstream sections with domestic counterparts (Lee) or to second language-specific sections with other international counterparts (Ayash, "Toward" 148). The unavoidable interactions among diverse domestic and international students or among international students themselves create a transnational configuration in these first-year writing courses.

Moving past the recognition and acknowledgement of the now inherent presence of transnationality in writing courses, it is imperative that instructors and administrators of transnational composition ponder how to foster the development of meaningful, beneficial, and transformative learning experiences in transnational classrooms. From our research findings, we argue that translingual practices can offer transnational composition viable pedagogical approaches and heuristics which enable students, irrespective of their linguistic and socio-cultural backgrounds, to navigate transnational spaces more effectively and arrive at fruitful educational experiences. Particularly, we argue that translingual practices are valuable in the way they afford students functioning in transnational spaces to better self-position, optimize their linguistic and cultural repertoires, and negotiate meaning-making.

Self-positioning

One major problem students face in transnational writing classrooms, as Ayash identifies, occurs when they need to reconcile the desire to "[preserve] their diverse language and semiotic resources" with the awareness that they still need to deliver "successful academic writings in the eyes of their teachers and other key gatekeepers" ("Toward" 8). Canagarajah describes his international students as having transnational "social and psychological affiliations" because they come from other countries and crossed borders both physically and figuratively ("Transnational" 5). Even his domestic students "inhabit transnational social fields" as they are exposed to other languages and cultures via media and technology (5). Since these student writers and readers enter the transnational composition classroom with diverse linguistic and cultural baggage, they have to grapple with dissimilar lexico-syntactic and rhetorical traditions in their repertoires to produce texts that can be accepted by and accessible to their instructors and peers who may come from differing sociolinguistic and cultural backgrounds.

Translingual practices, as evinced in the reviewed scholarship, can help both instructors and students tackle these dissonances. Many translingual assignments and activities have been designed to help student writers achieve more informed, effective *self-positioning*. That means a transnational social space fosters and encourages translingual writing but only if student resources are activated by knowledge of their positionality as transnational (and translingual) with linguistic and cultural affordances and resources. Caragarajah sees the literacy autobiography as an ideal assignment for transnational/translingual students because narrative autobiographical writing creates new knowledge and self-knowledge about the nature of students' translingual and transnational positions ("Transnational" 18). Sohan's relocalized listening practices enable students to see language difference as the norm, thereby encouraging them to draw upon all of their linguistic resources in their local language practices. These heuristics encourage students to take agency in their composing process, thus cultivating in them a stronger sense of self or identity. Additionally, different translingual assignments aim to expand students' self-awareness by motivating them to situate themselves in a writing ecology and scrutinize their relationship with this ecology, be it interpersonal or institutional (Ayash, "Toward" 151) or political and social (De Costa et al. 468). Embedded in these and other translingual practices is the cultivation of a translingual disposition as a pedagogical objective (e.g.; Lee and Jenks 320; Liao 758). A translingual disposition is crucial as it ensures that members of the classroom embrace a mindset open to linguistic and cultural diversity, which can prepare them for resolving conflicts caused by linguistic and cultural differences. From this vantage point, students can engage in transnational writing interactions with more confidence and clarity.

Optimizing Students' Diverse Linguistic and Cultural Repertoires

As mentioned above, the transnational space complexifies interactions and composing processes in first-year writing courses because any student, domestic or international alike, thanks to their dissimilar repertoires, contributes to the linguistic and cultural superdiversity in the classroom. Drawing on translingual pedagogical practices in such diverse contexts helps to reconcile linguistic and cultural dissonance and creates opportunities for students to recognize and utilize their repertoires in a generative fashion. All of the reviewed translingual assignments were designed with students' diverse language and culture backgrounds as points of departure and aimed at leveraging the linguistic, socio-cultural and semiotic affordances in their composing and communicating processes, enabling them to evolve into competent writers and communicators (e.g., De Costa et al.; Lee). For instance, reading response assignments that require engagement with code-meshed texts can help students discern dynamic and hybrid instances of language, challenging the assumption that there are monolithic standards and practices adhered to by all writers. Building on this recognition, students can negotiate meaning in their responses and, thereby, move beyond a conception that language practices and norms must remain fixed for meaningful communication. Likewise, multimedia assignments can motivate students to critically examine language norms and standards, and it can encourage students to draw upon their diverse repertoires. Lee's digital literacy narrative assignment, for instance, encourages students to mix multiple language genres and modes of delivery, with the result that students may come to better understand the diversity and wide array of differences in language use.

Sharpening Negotiation Skills

Transnational composition courses, as Donahue remarks, are "contact zones" ("The 'Trans'" 2) which are "social spaces where cultures meet, clash and grapple with each other" (Pratt 34). Being a member of a transnational space, one cannot avoid, but embrace negotiation as a key to successful interaction and communication (2). Translingual pedagogies allow for negotiations in a transnational first-year writing class to happen at different levels. Transnational writers –e.g. international students and others from different countries–write translingually because they negotiate first and second languages and cultures creatively and resourcefully. The student writer is constantly reminded of negotiating between the semiotic and linguistic affordances as well as rhetorical traditions of the languages/varieties they speak (Hanson 207; Lee 322). The Poetic Autoethnography project in Liao's course inspires students to negotiate cultural, semiotic, genre and stylistic differences (743). A critical translation sequence as the one in Ayash prompts students to consider their possible readership and negotiate their own affordances and those of the imagined audience ("Toward" 151). The sequence does not require students to produce "correct, accurate and quality writing" but negotiate and experiment various language options and generate solutions that help them "convey their intended meaning and functions" (148). Many translingual assignments create room for students to experiment with composing decisions, receive direct feedback from peers of different language and culture backgrounds and conduct several rounds of negotiations (e.g., Lee 321). These translingual assignments offer what Donahue calls "rhetorical and linguistic flexibility" to respond to and capitalize on the norms of multilingualism and multiculturalism in transnational contexts ("The Trans-" 3).

Implications for Future Directions

While translingual pedagogies have much to offer transnational first-year writing, it is necessary to also examine the issues for which translingualism has been challenged by scholars in other fields, such as applied linguistics, education, and L2 writing. Such an inquiry can result in a more nuanced understanding of the contribution and directions for the advancement of translingual pedagogies to transnational composition.

Looking at the pedagogical objectives of the reviewed courses, it is apparent that instructors addressed different writing issues rather than language acquisition and development. However, it has been well-documented in scholarship that language proficiency needs to be attended to. In her dialogue with Dwight Atkinson, Christine Tardy straightforwardly states that "...my students ask for [language instructions], and I see their successes in learning how to manipulate and exploit language, learning how to identify patterns, and learning how to vary patterns" (88). Dryer and Mitchell acknowledge the needs of multilingual students in their FYW course, which reflects "[students'] deeply ingrained assumption" that "engaging language issues means learning about languages" (140). Carol Severino recounts her learning experience grappling with Chinese and Spanish and argues strongly for instructors' special attention to assisting learners' acquisition processes (27-28). These scholars have testified to students' expectation to be taught language, including language norms, which goes against the philosophical principles of translingualism, a field that primarily confronts language norms and advocates norm negotiation. But even this core tenet of translingualism was challenged by Dwight Atkinson, who states "Language cannot be primarily about negotiating form. It's about expressing and negotiating meaning within form or through form" (Atkinson and Tardy 88). Atkinson further qualifies his stance by saying that "you can only express your individuality in forms invented by others" and "To be an individual, you have to do so in forms and practices which aren't your creation or about you especially" (88), stressing the indispensable role of forms in language production and meaning-making. Nevertheless, *no* articles in the selected literature include any discussion about how formal use of language was addressed within a translingual FYW course.

Nonetheless, existing scholarship does provide suggestions on how translingual practitioners can teach for students' language development. For example, discourse on language issues can be found in publications focusing on basic writing - not FYW - in which the instructors adopted a translingual approach. In her basic writing course for multilingual students, Sarah Stanley applies the *self-initiated focus on forms* approach originating from the field of second language acquisition to make students notice and then negotiate errors in their own writings and their peers' (39). Through this practice, Stanley elaborates on the translingual disposition on errors that calls for a change in the way instructors read students' errors/mistakes, encouraging them to differentiate errors from mistakes and view errors as zones for teacher-student negotiations (40). Stanley also relies on Canagarajah's definition of errors as intentional translanguaging choices that "fail to gain uptake" or "are not effectively negotiated for meaning" (42). In addition, Rashi Jain recounts four class snippets in which she drew students' attention to the dialectal differences of certain expressions and prompted them to reflect on their language and cultural experience, enabling them to further understand the dynamics in meaning and use of those expressions

(498-507). Obviously, the two translingual pedagogies described by Stanley and Jain focus on error treatment in students' language use, and these scholars propose a relatively fluid approach in conceptualizing errors as it invites students' negotiating input. While this approach has been applied in basic writing courses, instructors of transnational FYW courses could modify and adapt it to address grammatical or language issues made by more linguistically advanced student populations.

Another pedagogical issue about which scholars in other fields have interrogated translingualism is the need to teach for *transfer*. Referring to one common scenario encountered by students – "an introductory class with 300 students, where a TA is grading the paper on a rubric given to them by the professor," Tardy concludes that "[students] don't have opportunities to radically negotiate the discourses they're using. They probably need to get as close to the expectations as possible" (Atkinson and Tardy 88). Here, Tardy highlights the importance of teaching the normal writing conventions which students could transfer to their writing in other disciplinary classes and problematizes the call for challenging and negotiating the norms inherent in a translingual approach. The problem of transfer does not cease inside the school gate but looms large in the professional world after students complete their academic education. According to Ayash, monolingual norms are endorsed in the job market in Lebanon, countering translingual practices that academic contexts promote ("Hi-ein" 99). However, *no* selected publication articulates how a translingual pedagogy carries out the task of teaching for transfer as students graduate from the English class and enter other academic or professional spaces which may require them to communicate in English in standardized fashion.

Christine Tardy suggests a direction for translingual pedagogues to address transfer in their teaching, claiming that they "need to be engaging students with when [students] can make those negotiations, and when it carries risk—in what kinds of writing, what kinds of setting, with which teachers and tasks" (Atkinson and Tardy 88). Donahue also lays out how the notion of transfers has been studied in second language and foreign language research, and invites language specialists teaching in globalized, superdiverse contexts (translingual workers included) to consult such a body of works ("We" 136-138).

Finally, instructors and administrators of transnational first-year writing might also consider the pedagogical implications and blueprints provided in the scholarship on translingual theorization. Here, we would like to summarize one such publication, "Toward a Translingual Composition" by Brian Ray, which offers several activities that may be of interest to instructors looking for additional ways of implementing a translingual pedagogy in a transnational FYW course. One activity, for instance, requires that students introduce, explain, and illustrate a proverb from their L1 with examples. For L2 students, this requires that they translate the saying into English, which, as the author notes, can be a springboard for rich class discussions about how best to paraphrase the message for a wide range of audiences. As Ray points out, this activity can also help to raise student awareness about how using multiple languages can assist in the generation of ideas. In another assignment--a "transmedia activity"—students should adapt a story or fable by using alternative codes and literary practices. This could include using code-meshing or re-mediating a text to another medium and channel, such as Facebook or a blog. The author suggests having students select a brief story, such as one of Aesop's Fables. Next, students expand on the story by making adaptations to the language, by applying their own literary practices, or by revising the setting of the story to give it a more contemporary feel. This transmedia assignment can encourage students to draw upon the full range of their linguistic repertoire rather than restricting them to standard English practices.

Conclusion

Over the years, translingualism has offered an array of theoretical and pedagogical approaches that can be advantageously adopted in transnational composition contexts. The application of translingualism to this context is fitting since a transnational classroom can be defined as one in which students from around the world bring linguistic and cultural diversity. Indeed, students, with their multiple linguistic and cultural resources are already translingual to some extent and able to cross national borders both literally and figuratively. In other words, these translingual students do comprise and compose a transnational classroom. The translingual assignments and heuristics in our study exhibit various ways to tap into students' abundant linguistic and cultural repertoires, enabling them to develop a translingual/transnational disposition as well as effectively self-position and negotiate difference in the transnational composition classroom. Besides the fruitful intersections between translingualism and transnationalism, the review also indicates exploratory directions for translingual pedagogies. Specifically, we highlight the need for translingual/transnational practitioners to address language acquisition and developmental issues faced by multilingual writers and to teach for *transfer* with the understanding that first-year composition graduates, later on, will enter disciplinary and professional writing contexts that are not ready for norm negotiations as in translingual/transnational writing classrooms. Finally, we encourage translingual and transnational composition pedagogues to look into a large pool of translingual pedagogical implications in the scholarship and experiment and validate these implications in actual classrooms. Further explorations of these territories will result in an expanded repository of translingual pedagogies, which, in turn, will allow translingual/transnational practitioners to accommodate a wider range of students' writing needs.

Works Cited

Atkinson, Dwight., and Christine M. Tardy. "SLW at the Crossroads: Finding a Way in the Field." *Journal of Second Language Writing*, vol. 42, 2018, pp. 86–93.

Atkinson, Dwight., et al. "Clarifying the Relationship between L2 Writing and Translingual Writing: an Open Letter to Writing Studies Editors and Organization Leaders." *College English*, vol. 77, no. 4, 2015, pp. 383–389.

Ayash, Nancy Bou. *Toward Translingual Realities in Composition*. Utah State University Press, 2019.

—. "Hi-ein, Hi وهي or وهي Hi? Translingual Practices from Lebanon and mainstream literacy education". *Literacy as translingual practice: Between communities and classrooms*, edited by In Suresh A. Canagarajah, Routledge, 2013, pp. 96–103.

Canagarajah, A. Suresh. "Negotiating Translingual Literacy: An Enactment." *Research in the Teaching of English*, vol. 48, no. 1, 2013, pp. 40–7.

—. "Translingual Writing and Teacher Development in Composition." *College English*, vol. 78, no. 3, 2016, pp. 265–273.

—. *Transnational literacy autobiographies as translingual writing*. Routledge, 2019.

Chen, Xin. "Translingual practices in the first-year international students' English academic writing." *INTESOL Journal*, vol. 14, no.1, 2017, pp. 25–50.

De Costa, Peter., et al. "Pedagogizing Translingual Practice: Prospects and Possibilities." *Research in the Teaching of English*, vol. 51, no. 4, 2017, pp. 464–472.

Donahue, Christiane. "'Internationalization' and Composition Studies: Reorienting the Discourse." *College Composition and Communication*, vol. 61, no. 2, 2009, pp. 212–243.

—. "The 'Trans' in Transnational-Translingual: Rhetorical and Linguistic Flexibility as New Norms." *Composition Studies*, vol. 44, no. 1, 2016, pp. 147–150.

—. "We Are the 'Other': The Future of Exchanges between Writing and Language Studies." *Across the Disciplines*, vol. 15, no. 3, 2018, p. 130–143.

Dryer, Dylan B., and Paige Mitchell. "Seizing an Opportunity for Translingual FYC at the University of Maine: Provocative Complexities, Unexpected Consequences." *Crossing Divides: Exploring Translingual Writing Pedagogies and Programs*, edited by Bruce Horner and Laura Tetreault, University Press of Colorado, 2017, pp. 135–160.

Gallagher, Chris., and Matt Noonan. "BECOMING GLOBAL: Learning to "Do" Translingualism." *Crossing Divides: Exploring Translingual Writing Pedagogies and Programs*, edited by, edited by Bruce Horner and Laura Tetreault, University Press of Colorado, 2017, pp. 161–180.

Guerra, Juan C. "Cultivating a Rhetorical Sensibility in the Translingual Writing Classroom." *College English*, vol. 78, no. 3, 2016, pp. 228–233.

Hanson, Joleen. "Moving out of the Monolingual Comfort Zone and into the Multilingual World: An Exercise for the Writing Classroom." *Literacy as Translingual Practice: Between Communities and Classrooms*, edited by Suresh Canagarajah, Routledge, 2013, pp. 207–214.

Horner, Bruce. "Teaching Translingual Agency in Iteration: Rewriting Difference." *Crossing Divides: Exploring Translingual Writing Pedagogies and Programs*, edited by Bruce Horner and Laura Tetreault, University Press of Colorado, 2017, pp. 87–98.

Horner, Bruce., and John Trimbur. "English Only and U.S. College Composition." *College Composition and Communication*, vol. 53, no. 4, 2002, pp. 594–630.

Horner, Bruce., and Min-Zhan Lu. "Resisting monolingualism in 'English': Reading and writing the politics of language." *Rethinking English in schools: Towards a new and constructive stage*, edited by Carol Fox, Brian Street, and Viv Ellis, A&C Black, 2007, pp. 141–157.

—. "Translingual Literacy, Language Difference, and Matters of Agency." *College English*, vol. 75, no. 6, 2013, pp. 582–607.

Horner, Bruce., and Laura Tetreault. "Translation as (Global) Writing." *Composition Studies*, vol. 44, no. 1, 2016, p. 13-30.

Horner, Bruce., et al. "Toward a Multilingual Composition Scholarship: From English Only to a Translingual Norm." *College Composition and Communication*, vol. 63, no. 2, 2011, pp. 269–300.

Institute of International Education. Open Doors 2019, 2019. Retrieved from https://www.iie.org/en/Why-IIE/Announcements/2019/11/Number-of-International-Students-in-the-United-States-Hits-All-Time-High

Jain, Rashi. "Global Englishes, Translinguistic Identities, and Translingual Practices in a Community College ESL Classroom: A Practitioner Researcher Reports." *TESOL Journal*, vol. 5, no. 3, 2014, pp. 490–522.

Kilfoil, Carrie. "What's the Difference Between "Translingual" and "Transnational" Composition?: Clarifying the Relationship between two Terms" *Transnational Writing: A Blog for the Transnational Composition Group at the Conference on College Composition and Communication*, 9 September 2016, https://transnationalwriting.wordpress.com> Accessed 11 November. 2020

Kiernan, Julia., et al. "Translingual Approaches to Reading and Writing: Centering Students' Languages and Cultures within Reflective Practices of Translation." *L1 Educational Studies in Language and Literature*, vol. 17, 2017, pp. 1–18.

Lee, Jerry Won., and Christopher Jenks. "Doing Translingual Dispositions." College Composition and Communication, vol. 68, no.2, 2016, pp. 317–44.

Lee, Melissa E. "Shifting to the World Englishes Paradigm by Way of the Translingual Approach: Code-meshing as a Necessary Means of Transforming Composition Pedagogy." *TESOL Journal*, vol. 5, no. 2, 2014, pp. 312–329.

Liao, Fang-yu. "Translingual Pedagogy Through Poetry Writing: A Case of College Composition Courses." *Journal of Global Literacies, Technologies, and Emerging Pedagogies*, vol. 4, no. 3, 2018, pp. 741–765.

Lueck, Amy., and Shyam Sharma. "Writing a Translingual Script: Closed Captions in the English Multilingual Hearing Classroom." *Kairos*, vol. 17, no. 3, 2013.

Martín, Cristina S., et al. "Pedagogies of Digital Composing through a Translingual Approach." *Computers and Composition*, vol. 52, 2019, pp. 142–157.

Martins, David S., editor. *Transnational writing program administration*. University Press of Colorado, 2015.

Matsuda, Paul Kei. "The Lure of Translingual Writing." *PMLA*, vol. 129, no. 3, 2014, pp. 478–483.

Pratt, Mary Louise. "Arts of the Contact Zone." *Profession*, 1991, pp. 33–40.

Ray, Brian. *Toward a Translingual Composition: Ancient Rhetorics and Language Difference*. 2012. University of North Carolina at Greensboro, PhD dissertation.

Rose, Shirley K., and Irwin Weiser. "Introduction: Internationalized Writing Programs in the Twenty-First-Century United States." *The Internationalization of US Writing Programs*, edited by Shirley K. Rose and Irwin Weiser, Utah State UP, 2018, pp. 3–18.

Severino, Carol. "'Multilingualizing' Composition: A Diary Self-Study of Learning Spanish and Chinese." *Composition Studies*, vol. 45, no. 2, 2017, pp. 12–31.

Shapiro, Shawna., et al. "Teaching for Agency: From Appreciating Linguistic Diversity to Empowering Student Writers." *Composition Studies*, vol. 44, no. 1, 2016, pp. 31–52.

Sohan, Vanessa Kraemer. "Relocalized Listening: Responding to All Student Texts from a Translingual Starting Point." *Reworking English in Rhetoric and Composition: Global Interrogations, Local Interventions*, edited by Bruce Horner and Karen Kopelson, SIU Press, 2014, pp. 191–206.

Stanley, Sarah. "Noticing the Way: Translingual Possibility and Basic Writers." *Journal of Basic Writing*, vol. 32, no. 1, 2013, pp. 37–61.

Tardy, Christine. "Crossing or creating divides? A plea for transdisciplinary scholarship." *Crossing divides: Exploring translingual writing pedagogies and programs*, edited by Bruce Horner and Laura Tetreault, University Press of Colorado, 2017, pp. 181–189.

Vertovec, Steven. "Super-Diversity and Its Implications." *Ethnic and Racial Studies*, vol. 30, no. 6, 2007, pp. 1024–1054.

Wang, Zhaozhe. "Rethinking Translingual as a Transdisciplinary Rhetoric: Broadening the Dialogic Space." *Composition Forum*, vol. 40, 2018, http://www.compositionforum.com/issue/40/translingual.php. Accessed 11 November 2020.

You, Xiaoye, editor. *Transnational writing education: Theory, history, and practice*. Routledge, 2018.

Afterword

The goal of *Creating a Transnational Space in the First-Year Writing Classroom* is to offer pedagogical methods and results of applied praxis to those interested in establishing and/or cultivating transnational spaces in first-year composition. While much has been contributed to the development of transnational rhetoric as theory, there has been relatively little work with the sole purpose of offering educators theoretical and practical means of achieving this goal. The volume addresses the successes and shortcomings of course designs, assignment designs, and ethnographic research. Several chapters in the work offer unique perspectives from writing program administrators, graduate teaching assistants, course developers, and instructors.

While *Creating a Transnational Space in the First-Year Writing Classroom* extends our knowledge of applied transnational pedagogy, it invokes further study of other rhetorical factors involved in teaching first-year writing such as digital access, government and university policy, and visual rhetorics to name a few. The volume addresses two facets of Xiaoye You's foundation of transnationalism (translingualism and transculturalism) but does not offer significant insight into cosmopolitanism and its effect on pedagogical research. Future research in the field of transnational pedagogy might also consider alternative pedagogies that incorporate problem and inquiry-based learning, simulation activities, backward design theory, and other active learning frameworks.

While we encourage further research, we believe the pedagogical theories and applications provided make this volume especially valuable to the field of transnational rhetoric. The diversity of perspectives and research methods in this volume offers valuable insight for all stakeholders involved in creating, executing, evaluating first-year writing courses.

Author Biographies

Chapter 1 - Erasing the Idea of Monolingual Students in Translingual Spaces: A Study of Translingual Pedagogy in First-Year Writing

Norma Denae Dibrell is a former high school English teacher and current first-year writing lecturer at the University of Texas at Rio Grande Valley. She is a native of the Rio Grande Valley. Her research interests include transfer, translingualism, feminist theory, first-year writing studies, cultural rhetoric and decolonial studies.

Chapter 2 - Translanguaging and Academic Writing: Possibilities and Challenges in English-Only Classrooms

Abu Saleh Mohammad Rafi is a PhD candidate in Linguistics at James Cook University, Australia. He has been exploring the promises of translanguaging pedagogical approaches in the context of Bangladeshi higher education. Previously, he studied Sociolinguistics at Liverpool Hope University, United Kingdom.

Anne-Marie Morgan Professor and Dean of the College of Arts, Society and Education at James Cook University in Australia. She has over 25 years of experience working with teachers of languages in schools and universities. Her research interests include plurilingualism, translanguaging as classroom pedagogy, the teaching of languages including English, and the work of teachers in engaging with the diversity of student cohorts. She has over 50 major publications and has conducted more than 20 major research projects into languages education as Chief Investigator, including two current projects with the Australian Government and the Australian Research Council.

Chapter 3 - Language, Home, and Transnational Space

Dr. Naoko Akai-Dennis obtained a PhD in English and Education from Columbia University Graduate School of Arts and Sciences. Her research interests are the relationship between language and self, autobiography as an inquiry, storytelling, and teaching of writing. Theoretically she is persuaded by post-colonial theory, post-structural feminist theory, and started to delve into post-humanist theory. She currently teaches College Writing I, College Writing II, College Writing I paired with Integrated ELL Level 3 Learning Community course, and an accelerated cluster Writing Skills II and College Writing for Early College Program at Bunker Hill Community College, Massachusetts, as an assistant professor of English. She enjoys and appreciates the diverse community of students, staff, and professors at the college.

Chapter 4 - A Confluence of Xings: A Nested Heuristic for Developing and Networking Individual, Programmatic, and Institutional Spaces of Transnational Work

Andrew Hollinger has taught at The University of Texas Rio Grande Valley (formally UTPA) since 2012 in the Department of Language & Writing Studies, and has been the WPA for the first-year writing program since 2015. He teaches primarily first-year composition and technical communication where his previous experience as a high school teacher allows him to work closely with students transitioning from K12 or career paths into the university. His work focuses on writing pedagogy, writing administration, event theories and design, genre, and materiality.

Colin Charlton graduated with a PhD in English and a specialization in Rhetoric & Composition from Purdue University in 2005. He has taught at The University of Texas Rio Grande Valley (formerly UTPA) since 2005, where he has been the Department Chair of Writing & Language Studies since 2015. He teaches at all levels, but really enjoys his work in transitional and first-year writing courses and teacher training courses at the upper-undergraduate and graduate levels. His research includes writing pedagogy, event theories and design thinking, and (writing program) administration.

Chapter 5 - All Writers have more Englishes to Learn: Translingual First-Year Composition classes' Promotion of Composition's Threshold Concepts

A PhD student at the University of Texas at El Paso, **Asmita Ghimire** holds a Master of Arts in English from Tribhuvan University, Nepal and Master in English, Linguistics and Writing from the University of Minnesota Duluth. She was invited to the Young Scholar program organized by the British Academy of Writing 2018 where she presented and published "The Other Side of Afghan War: Women, War and the Question of Social Injustice." Focusing on transnational and translingual writing, she and Wright are publishing a special edition of Academic Labor: Research and Artistry.

Professor at the University of Minnesota Duluth, **Elizabethada A. Wright** teaches in the Department of English, Linguistics, and Writing Studies and is a member of the faculty at the University of Minnesota Twin Cities' Literacy and Rhetorical Studies Program. She has published in Rhetoric Society Quarterly, Rhetoric Review, College English Association Critic, Studies in the Literary Imagination, as well as in a number of other journals and books.

Chapter 6 - Translingual and Transnational Pedagogies Enacted: Linguistic and Cultural Trajectory Narratives in First-Year Composition

Demet Yigitbilek is a PhD student in English Studies at Illinois State University (ISU) where she mainly designs and teaches FYC, theming them around what excites her at the time. Her research interests center around translingualism and linguistic diversity in Applied Linguistics, Second Language Writing, and Composition Studies. Her teaching is greatly influenced by her transnational identity as a Turkish scholar who has taught in Spain, Turkey and now in the US higher education. She enjoys experimenting with new ideas and pushes students to think beyond the walls of the classroom. So far, she has taught FYC as Language and Identity, Critical Writer-Researchers, and Composing In/Of Our Lives.

Chapter 7 - Learning by Writing: Possibilities of Tele-Collaborative Transnational Education In and Beyond a First-Year Writing Classroom

Ekaterina Gradaleva is an Associate Professor at Samara State Technical University. She is a graduate of Samara State University with a Doctorate in Germanic Languages. At present, she lectures EFL and Business English at the Department of Linguistics, Cross-Cultural Communication and Russian as a Foreign Language, and serves as a scientific mentor supervising student research in Linguistics and Business Studies. Her research interests involve Cultural Studies, Professional Communication, Project-Based Learning, and Teaching English for Specific Purposes.

Maria Houston is an English Faculty member at Texas A&M University in Texarkana. Maria currently teaches courses in Digital Writing and is in process of designing a Business Course with a focus on professional communication and cultural intelligence. She has an extensive record of publications in Second Language Literacy, Transnational Pedagogy, Collaborative Programming and Transnational Digital Rhetoric and Communications.

Chapter 8 - Investigating Translingual Practices in First-Year Writing Courses: Implications for Transnational Composition Pedagogies

Phuong Minh Tran is a PhD Candidate in Second Language Studies/ESL at Purdue University. Her research encompasses second language writing, intercultural competence in writing studies, transnational composition pedagogies, Backward Design in curricular development and World Englishes. Phuong is a member of the Transculturation in Introductory Composition project which focuses on intercultural competence development in first-year writing students and which has received several internal and external grants, including the CWPA Research Grant from the Council of Writing Program

Administrators in 2018. Phuong's work on cultural studies can be found in the edited collection Building a Community, Having a Home: A History of the Conference on College Composition and Communication Asian/Asian American Caucus (2017). Her other publications are forthcoming in the Journal of World Englishes and the edited collection Teaching and Studying Transnational Composition. At Purdue, Phuong is an instructor of mainstream and L2-specific First-Year Writing and Professional Writing.

Kyle J. Lucas is a PhD student in the English Department at Purdue University. His research focuses on the use of genre analysis and corpus linguistics to analyze student and professional academic writing. He is particularly interested in analyzing and comparing the rhetorical structures of research articles across academic disciplines. His most recent project involves English for Specific Purposes research in the field of philosophy. Other research interests include the role of critical thinking instruction in English for Academic Purposes curriculum as well as how genre-based and corpus-based analytical approaches can be used as pedagogical methods in English for Specific Purposes and English for Academic Purposes classrooms.

Kenneth Tanemura is a PhD Candidate in Second Language Studies/ESL at Purdue University. His research focuses on motivation in heritage language and L2 learning, and particularly how the L2 motivational self-system as conceptualized by Dörnyei can measure stages of learning. Kenneth is currently involved in various collaborative, duoethnographic projects about disciplinary identity and motivation in L2 researchers, specifically how scholars are motivated to investigate the integration of disability studies in the L2 writing syllabus, and the motivation to explore and analyze motivation itself as a subfield of applied linguistics. He also has work forthcoming in the Journal of World Englishes.

Index

www.ingramcontent.com/pod-product-compliance
Lightning Source LLC
Chambersburg PA
CBHW050513280326
41932CB00014B/2302